Advocating Digital Citizenship

Advocating Digital Citizenship

Resources for the Library and Classroom

Carrie Rogers-Whitehead,
Amy O. Milstead,
and Lindi Farris-Hill

LIBRARIES
UNLIMITED®

An Imprint of ABC-CLIO, LLC
Santa Barbara, California • Denver, Colorado

Library of Congress Cataloging-in-Publication Data

Names: Rogers-Whitehead, Carrie, 1983– author. | Milstead, Amy O., author. | Farris-Hill, Lindi, author.
Title: Advocating digital citizenship : resources for the library and classroom / Carrie Rogers-Whitehead, Amy O. Milstead, and Lindi Farris-Hill.
Description: Santa Barbara, California : Libraries Unlimited, [2022] | Includes bibliographical references and index.
Identifiers: LCCN 2022017637 (print) | LCCN 2022017638 (ebook) | ISBN 9781440878893 (paperback) | ISBN 9781440878909 (ebook)
Subjects: LCSH: Citizenship—Study and teaching—United States. | Digital media—Study and teaching—United States. | Internet in education—United States. | School libraries—Information technology—United States. | Online etiquette—Study and teaching—United States. | Information society—Moral and ethical ethics—United States. | BISAC: LANGUAGE ARTS & DISCIPLINES / Library & Information Science / General | LANGUAGE ARTS & DISCIPLINES / Library & Information Science / Digital & Online Resources
Classification: LCC LC1091 .R72 2022 (print) | LCC LC1091 (ebook) | DDC 370.11/5—dc23/eng/20220616
LC record available at https://lccn.loc.gov/2022017637
LC ebook record available at https://lccn.loc.gov/2022017638

ISBN: 978-1-4408-7889-3 (paperback)
      978-1-4408-7890-9 (ebook)

26 25 24 23 22   1 2 3 4 5

This book is also available as an eBook.

Libraries Unlimited
An Imprint of ABC-CLIO, LLC

ABC-CLIO, LLC
147 Castilian Drive
Santa Barbara, California 93117
www.abc-clio.com

This book is printed on acid-free paper ∞

Manufactured in the United States of America

ISTE Standards for Students. ISTE Standards for Students, © 2021, ISTE® (International Society for Technology in Education), iste.org. All rights reserved. Reprinted with permission.

Contents

Introduction: The Role of Digital Citizenship in Libraries and Schools

In 2016, I had just started my company, Digital Respons-Ability, and had the opportunity to travel to San Francisco to attend the second annual "DigCit Summit" at Twitter Headquarters. During breakfast when I chatted with others and throughout the day, I kept running into people who were media specialists or had some kind of library background. Near the end of the day, I was on a panel on stage and I asked how many people in the audience were current or former librarians. My suspicions from earlier conversations were confirmed when many hands shot up in the crowd.

Librarians have been involved in digital citizenship since the beginning of the discipline's movement—in fact even more so. I've half-joked with others that "I did digital citizenship before I knew there was a term digital citizenship." Perhaps that's you as well, and when you read this book, you may nod your head thinking, "Oh yes, I knew that" or "I've done that before." This book is written by a former public librarian and two current school librarians—all of whom have taught and advocated for digital citizenship before they were familiar with the term. Hopefully, by the end of this book, you will not only be familiar with the term and concepts behind it, but you'll be ready to teach and advocate on your own.

What Is Digital Citizenship?

Digital citizenship can be defined as the ethical and responsible use of technology. But that is just the most basic definition. Digital citizenship is an umbrella term that encompasses concepts like being healthy online, civic and political online engagement, communication, media literacy, and online safety. There are continuing conversations and continuing evolution about this complex and multidisciplinary concept. However, most stakeholders, international organizations, and educators use the term "digital citizenship."

Dr. Mike Ribble, author of *Digital Citizenship in Schools*, 3rd edition, articulated nine specific elements of digital citizenship, which are included in this book:

- Digital access
- Digital commerce
- Digital communication
- Digital literacy

- Digital etiquette

- Digital law

- Digital rights and responsibilities

- Digital health and wellness

- Digital safety and security (Ribble, 2015)

A holistic, broad framework must be used when discussing digital citizenship. One needs all the elements to be a full and participating digital citizen. For example, you can't be safe online unless you have basic literacy skills to change controls, report inappropriate content and curate your own consumption. And you can't be a digital citizen at all if you don't have consistent and/or high-speed access to the Internet.

The International Society for Technology in Education (ISTE) is a non-profit organization serving educators in over 100 countries interested in and/or working with technology in the educational field. It provides professional learning, resources, an annual ed tech event, peer-reviewed journals, books, and more to support professionals and technology in education. ISTE creates standards for students and teachers on working with technology, including digital citizenship. Many state- and district-level standards are based on ISTE.

Formed in 1979 originally as the International Council for Computers in Education, ISTE has not only changed their name but their focus over the years. In 1998, the original Technology Foundation Standards for Students were created. These original standards were focused more on basic digital literacy skills. But over the two decades since ISTE has adapted their standards to not just cover the understanding of technology but the application and use of technology in one's life as well (ISTE, n.d.).

ISTE has a holistic approach with five competencies for students:

- Inclusive: I'm open to hearing and respectfully recognizing multiple viewpoints and I engage with others online with respect and empathy.

- Balanced: I make informed decisions about how to prioritize my time and activities online and off.

- Informed: I evaluate the accuracy, perspective, and validity of digital media and social posts.

- Engaged: I use technology and digital channels for civic engagement, to solve problems and be a force for good in both physical and virtual communities.

- Alert: I am aware of my online actions and know how to be safe and create safe spaces for others online. (ISTE, n.d.)

ISTE also has standards for students, one of them being a "digital citizen." They state that for students to be a digital citizen, they need to "recognize the rights, responsibilities, and opportunities of living, learning and working in an interconnected digital world, and they [need to] act and model in ways that are safe, legal and ethical." Other ISTE student standards can fall under this digital citizenship umbrella such as being a "computational thinker" or a "global collaborator" (ISTE, n.d.). You can also find digital citizenship in the Common Core and interwoven in the American Association of School Librarians (AASL) standards (AASL, 2021).

Harvard's Berkman Klein Institute recently proposed using the term "digital citizenship+," where the plus symbol indicates it's a word with broad scope and complexity. They note in their March 2020 report that "over the past two decades we have seen the emergence of a range of digital citizenship frameworks, addressing relevant skills that aim to help young people critically, ethically, and effectively use digital technologies" (Cortesi et al., 2020). Through their research they "selected and studied" 35 frameworks around the umbrella of digital citizenship, and from those frameworks they narrowed down four interconnected clusters: participation, empowerment, engagement, and well-being on where those concepts fell (Cortesi et al., 2020).

Whatever standards/clusters you focus on in your library, there are commonalities between them all. The standards referenced in this book all have similar themes:

- Digital citizenship is holistic.

- Digital citizenship instruction should be student/youth centered.

- Digital citizenship instruction should address and build skills.

- Digital citizenship is participatory and engaging. (ISTE, n.d.)

This book will focus on digital citizenship concepts, standards, and frameworks—but to help librarians teach and advocate for skills. The term skills, sometimes referred to as "literacies" or "competencies," refers to the application of knowledge (Cortesi et al., 2020). It's not enough to know about digital citizenship—one needs to apply that knowledge. Someone who is an empowered digital citizen has the literacy skills to use technology, can examine their attitudes and values, and then shift their behavior in their online life. Librarians are involved in the work of helping, educating, and changing their communities. And that education and change should go beyond the walls of the library. The goal of the lesson plans, program outlines, and details of this book is for patrons to develop digital citizenship skills and use them in their schooling, workplace, and everyday life.

Why Should Librarians Be Involved in Digital Citizenship?

I shouldn't have been so surprised to see so many librarians or former librarians at Twitter HQ that day in 2016; librarians have always been involved in digital citizenship. Librarians are trained in media literacy, and being able to navigate and evaluate information is one core skill of digital citizenship. They also typically have more flexibility in their role, and digital citizenship is one of those responsibilities that naturally falls on their desk. All librarians are at the frontlines of technology. They are the ones helping with computers, working with young people in free and informal moments where technology is involved, answering questions on software, databases, and so much more. Ask your public or school librarian who tweens are following, what apps are popular or the latest online game, and they'll probably have an answer.

School librarians (or media specialists) are often the only position in a school that has specific Common Core or other standards related to digital citizenship. Twenty-first-century librarians are greatly involved in technology; many media specialists are the technology coordinator/trainer/troubleshooter and librarian all in one. Media specialists are the ones running around the school implementing new technology, assisting teachers, instructing on technology, and much more. They do all of this in addition to traditional library responsibilities such as collection development and reference.

Public libraries are what is known as "third space." Evelyn Delgado, in a 2020 article in *Public Libraries*, writes, "Prominent child development theorists suggest that the place where children learn can be considered a third 'teacher' and that public libraries are well-positioned to address this need, creating lifelong relationships with children and their caregivers and providing children with opportunities to help them grow and develop" (Delgado, 2020). Public libraries are a free, open, and public space where people voluntarily go—one of a dwindling amount of this type of free and open space in the United States. "It is in these spaces where communities are built," writes Delgado. It's also in these spaces where digital citizenship can be advocated and taught (Delgado, 2020).

Librarians and libraries should be involved in digital citizenship because it's not only their mission but because they have the opportunity. Librarians have flexibility in teaching and advocating, the trust the community gives them, and the spaces to make a difference. Digital citizenship involves a variety of professions and perspectives, but what's often lacking is the opportunity. It's not enough to talk and advocate for digital citizenship—you have to do it. You have to work directly with the populations you're advocating for. Librarians are on the ground doing the work and can shift norms, reach people, and play a vital role in the digital movement and guide where it will go.

History of Digital Citizenship

The digital citizenship movement is not owned by any one person or organization. It's grown both ground-up and sometimes top-down through educators, academics, librarians, and others. There's no "birth date" of digital citizenship, but the term began appearing in the late 1990s as more technology came into classrooms. In those early days, digital citizenship was focused on access to technology and the hard skills: digital literacy. Access in the late 1990s and 2000s was significantly smaller than now. Pew Research estimates that only half of adults were online in 2000 (Anderson & Horrigan, 2016).

An additional emphasis then was on the word "citizen." Discussions by academics and policy makers were around the need for the Internet and technology to be a fully participating citizen. The 2007 book *Digital Citizenship: The Internet, Society, and Participation* described the term as "the ability to participate in society online" (Mossberger et al., 2008). The book also conducted research around digital citizenship for participating in the economy. The authors found that individuals in the 21st-century knowledge economy had higher wages—and that those left out of this economy were increasingly divided from the rest of society. This discussion of access and the digital divide will be covered more in depth in Chapter 4.

Since the beginning of the digital citizenship movement, there have been concerns and conversations on online safety. The term "digital citizenship" is less familiar to most people than "online safety." In fact, many people equate digital citizenship with online safety, but that is a false equivocation. Digital safety and security fall under the overarching term "digital citizenship" (Ribble, 2015). Topics of online safety, like cyberbullying and sexting, are often the ones that grab headlines and attention. But it's important to remember that one cannot be safe online without other digital citizenship skills.

In recent years, particularly as schools have gone 1:1 with devices, there's been more of a student-centered approach to digital citizenship. Many have learned that simply saying, "No, that's unsafe" is unhelpful in a world with the Internet and screens everywhere and a knowledge economy that requires and rewards technology skills. Increasingly there are conversations about embedding digital citizenship across multiple subjects and at earlier ages. Digital citizenship cannot just be a one-off conversation once in a while. The new approach and standards to digital citizenship understand that technology is not a once-a-week discussion, but an everyday occurrence. School librarians are particularly vital to embedding digital citizenship across multiple classrooms, and strategies and practices will be shared in Chapters 5 to 7.

What does digital citizenship look like in 5 to 10 years? That's hard to answer, but there are broad technology trends that may influence the practice, like:

- Generational changes: Generation Z has used the Internet since they were young and are entering college and the workplace. The generation behind, the Alphas, has never existed in a world without social media and high-speed access, and in a few years, they will be the generation in middle school.

- Gaming: Online gaming has exploded in the last decade with a separate digital and media ecosystem of streamers and new influencers. Parents of Gen Zs and Alphas have had games since they were children and are now raising new generations of gamers.

- Remote learning and work: The COVID-19 pandemic accelerated the move to remote learning and work. There is more screen time than ever before.

- The techlash: The term "techlash" is a portmanteau of technology and backlash, and it's found bipartisan support and growth in recent years. There are lawsuits against Google, Facebook, Apple, and more. Government officials and other regulators have pushed back against Chinese tech companies. There is bipartisan support for more regulations around big technology companies. This techlash may influence laws, norms, privacy, and more in technology in future years.

A certainty of the future is change. Norms and values around technology are shifting. Technology is more integrated into our day-to-day lives. Processing speeds, artificial intelligence (AI), and other tech developments pose promise and pitfalls. Digital citizenship must continue to change and adapt as the rest of the world does.

What This Book Covers

This book seeks to prepare those librarians to be part of the digital citizenship movement and make impactful change. The first three chapters of the book discuss theory—educating on concepts, ideas, research, and more on digital citizenship and suggesting policies for library administrators. The early chapters provide a foundation for the rest of the book, where theory and policy turn into practice. If you feel comfortable with digital citizenship and its varied concepts and ideas, skip ahead and go straight to the programming and practice sections. Chapter 4 covers programming ideas for all ages, suggestions on advocacy, and details the role librarians play in digital inclusion. In Chapter 5 the book shifts its focus to school librarians, first addressing the needs of elementary students before moving to secondary students in Chapters 6 and 7. If you are an instructional technology specialist or in a role that educates teachers, page ahead to Chapter 7 for digital citizenship teaching practices. Librarians are busy; if you need a quick answer or a program idea, go to the back of the book to the appendixes. The appendixes also have outlines, templates, and other practical resources to use on the job. For librarians excited about the topic of digital citizenship and wanting deeper instruction, read over the detailed references at the back of the book.

Whatever your role in the library—youth services librarian, media specialist, instructional technology specialist, library assistant, library administrator, or more—digital citizenship affects you. This is a subject that is only going to grow in importance as the role of technology grows in our lives. *Advocating Digital Citizenship: Resources for the Library and Classroom* is written by librarians for librarians. We've been on the ground with students, parents, and educators and know how critical the skills of digital citizenship are in preparing students and creating a more equitable, responsible, and civil online society. You're probably on the ground too and may be familiar with digital citizenship. Now it's time to take that familiarity, learn more, and help create empowered and educated digital citizens.

CHAPTER 1

Media Literacy and Digital Law

For many across the United States, the January 6 insurrection at the Capitol was a wake-up call. The rioters came from different parts of the country and were members of distinctive groups—but all had a commonality: they were there because of false beliefs perpetuated and validated by different parts of the media. While media is just one factor for the unrest and dissent, it's an important one.

Turner Bitton, a journalist and the president of the Utah Center for Civic Improvement, said,

> Media literacy is the cornerstone of democracy in the 21st Century. Our democratic norms are being tested by the vast amount of information generated and propagated online. This stress test is compounded by the fact that many consumers of information demonstrate a limited ability to discern the quality and type of information they consume. In order to ensure that the norms that have made our country prosperous and safe continue, we must embrace the role each of us has as citizens online. Media literacy is the foundational skillset for doing so.

Even before January 6, more Americans were noticing hyper-partisanship and bias in media. Americans saw the media as playing an important role in the institutions we all share. In late 2020, the Gallup and Knight Foundation published a report of Americans' attitudes towards the news media. In a divided and often partisan landscape, the "vast majority of Americans (81%) say that, in general, the news media is 'critical' (42%) or 'very important' (39%) to democracy" (Knight Foundation, 2020). Partisanship continues to grow and a 2022 Knight Foundation poll found that "among Americans, 71% say the internet does more to divide us than bring us together" (Knight Foundation, 2022).

This chapter discusses media literacy, part of which includes digital law and digital rights and responsibilities. It also covers the recent technological and systemic changes which have made this topic even more urgent than ever. Librarians have always had a key role in educating and advocating for media literacy, and they are needed more than ever.

Librarians' Role in Media Literacy

There is more discussion about media literacy than ever before. That 2020 Gallup and Knight poll found that three in four Americans "say that the spread of misinformation online is 'a major problem'" (Knight Foundation, 2020). There is a push and a desire for more media literacy education with more government initiatives, like Media Literacy Now, addressing K–12 education at a state legislative level, and more think tanks and newsprint targeted at the issue.

People trust librarians to address media literacy. A presentation by Lee Rainie, director of Internet, science and technology research at the Pew Research Center, discussed how people want to find good information; they felt librarians could help them. Rainie showed a chart of where people trusted sources of information. "Information from local public library" was at the top of the chart, above "info from health care providers," "info from government sources," and even "info from family and friends" (Rainie, 2017). Rainie also cites surveys that found 77% of Americans think their local public library gives them the information they need (Rainie, 2017).

Librarians also may have more time than other educators to address media literacy instruction. In a 2020 report, the National Association of Media Literacy Education (NAMLE) surveyed members and educators and found that the two main challenges for media literacy instruction were "competing curricular requirements (50%)" and "lack of time (45%)" (NAMLE, 2020). Teachers in the classroom are often just trying to keep up with their requirements; adding further teaching in media literacy could be burdensome. Another issue in media literacy instruction is a lack of content and curriculum. There is also insufficient funding for media literacy. That funding is often tied in with other projects, such as those only addressing fake news or speaking to one particular age or demographic. There is not just one repository for media literacy curriculum; educators have to hunt among a variety of different resources and organizations.

Recently, however, there has been increased research and work in this area. Some sources librarians may find helpful in their hunts are:

- News Literacy Project
- News Co/Lab out of Arizona State University's Walter Cronkite School of Journalism and Mass Communication
- MediaWise
- NAMLE
- AllSides.org
- Center for Media Literacy
- Living Room Conversations
- Common Sense Media
- Pulitzer Center
- Media Education Lab
- KQED Teach Media Academy

In addition to the trust the public has in librarians to help them sort through information, librarians have mandates and requirements to follow. Those requirements, perhaps more than any other factor, make them the professionals best suited to help students—and the broader society—become media literate.

The American Association of School Librarians (AASL) wrote a set of *National School Library Standards for Learners, School Librarians, and School Libraries.* These standards, also written as a colorful Crosswalk to better compare and contrast, address media literacy from six different shared foundations: inquire, include, collaborate, curate, explore, and engage (AASL, 2021).

Common Core Standards, which are used in most states, include media literacy in the English language arts (ELA) standards. According to the Common Core main site, "The skills and knowledge captured in the ELA/literacy standards are designed to prepare students for life outside the classroom." Some of those standards address the "integration of knowledge and ideas" and require students to evaluate claims and content in media, examine different speakers' views, and use media to express information (National Governors Association Center for Best Practices, n.d.). States and school districts may also have their own specific standards on media literacy, and librarians should check locally on what is used in their school. In this book, International Society for Technology in Education (ISTE) student standards are used in sample and startup lessons. According to ISTE, the "ISTE Standards provide the competencies for learning, teaching and leading in the digital age, providing a comprehensive roadmap for the effective use of technology in schools worldwide" (ISTE, n.d.).

Some criticism and commentaries complain that media literacy is not more woven throughout the Common Core and school curriculum in general. Media literacy is not just found in ELA but also in health, science, computer science, history, and more. Another big concern is that in addition to this curriculum being spottily included in various subjects, it's left out of standardized testing. NAMLE reports that "since the No Child Left Behind Act (2001) and its successor, Every Student Succeeds Act (2015), K–12 schools have been pressured to meet external demands. In schools across the country, curriculum decisions focus on subjects that will be tested statewide and nationally. Media literacy may be an acknowledged need, but it is not on the list of subjects tested and therefore is simply not perceived as critical to the school curriculum as other areas" (NAMLE, 2020). Educators are busy, and if something is not a requirement, then it may simply be left out.

This gap in curriculum, funding, and testing requirements is one that librarians, both public and school, can fill. A school librarian may have more flexibility during the day than a student who is constantly with a group of students. They can also curate and pull together the large variety of media literacy content to make it easier for teachers to integrate it into the classroom.

Public librarians can also get involved to support media literacy competencies. The Common Core has an increased focus on nonfiction reading (Lschulte, 2014). Public librarians can organize and display well-reviewed nonfiction books and booklists for all ages. The standards also emphasize using primary sources and evaluating evidence. This is an opportunity for public libraries to share and showcase their online resources and databases, which have those sources. Public librarians can also meet with their school librarian counterparts on ways to support them. Perhaps it's a way to deliver books their way or to cross-promote media literacy–related programs. Whatever the method is, students are already missing media literacy education in many of their subjects, which increases the need for it to be reinforced in other environments.

The rest of this chapter and some appendixes will share specific ideas for librarians to integrate media literacy into the classroom or library. But what must first be addressed are definitions of the concept. NAMLE reports that "there is a lack of public understanding about what it means to be 'media literate'" (NAMLE, 2020). Just like with digital citizenship, media literacy is an umbrella term that encompasses a variety of skills and concepts. What are those concepts? How do they overlap with digital citizenship? And how does technology influence how we teach and talk about media literacy?

Media Literacy in the 21st Century

In 2018 I interviewed Michelle Lipkin, the director of the NAMLE, for my book *Digital Citizenship: Teaching Strategies and Practice from the Field*. In that conversation, she spoke about the connections between digital citizenship and media literacy. Lipkin spoke about how long media literacy has been around. It's an established practice found in multiple subjects and included in educator standards. "Concepts of media literacy originated many decades ago while digital citizenship is a really new concept," she said (Rogers-Whitehead, 2019).

It's that newness of digital citizenship that blurs the lines, differentiating factors, and overlap between the two disciplines. The newness, as well as the rapid pace of technology, makes it sometimes unclear what will happen next in both practices. Lipkin said of both disciplines, "It's super important that we work together because our goals—to ensure students are prepared to thrive in the media-saturated world—align so nicely together" (Rogers-Whitehead, 2019).

Digital citizenship is a part of media literacy. And media literacy is a part of digital citizenship. They are connected through the skills they teach: critical thinking, responsibly sharing and using information, evaluating resources, collaborating, and more. Media literacy contrasts with digital citizenship in that its area includes *all* media, not just content online. However, with more content online than ever before, that line can get blurry. Media literacy also has more established and agreed-upon standards. Digital citizenship includes topics like digital health and wellness, digital commerce, privacy, and more. However, there are parts of media literacy that include mental health, privacy, and evaluating financial transactions online. Digital commerce is part of digital citizenship, and it also relates to media literacy. For example, the ability to evaluate Internet ads and potential scams is part of having both digital commerce and media literacy skills. As technology has increased, these two fields have overlapped more, and as Lipkin recommends, we all need to work together.

Technology Trends and Media Literacy

We all have seen the growth of content and media in our lifetimes. Librarians reading this book may remember card catalogs and rows and rows of magazines and journals to be retrieved by inquiring students. Technology has changed all our lives and how we talk and teach about media literacy. How we find information has changed. There are fewer gatekeepers and arbiters of truth. The new gatekeepers are algorithms. Those algorithms come from search engines, social media feeds, YouTube channels, and e-commerce sites. Those algorithms are not always even understood by their creators. In an article out of *Futurism*, author Bahar Gholipour writes, "It's difficult to figure out if an algorithm is biased or fair, even for computer experts. One reason is that the details behind an algorithm's creation are often considered proprietary information . . . in more advanced cases, the algorithms are so complex that even their creators don't know exactly how they work. This is AI's so-called black box problem—our inability to see the inside of an algorithm and understand how it arrives at a decision" (Gholipour, 2018).

Humans, like many algorithms, have biases. These biases by human-created content have contributed to the erosion of trust in the media. Gatekeepers are not necessarily a negative thing—gatekeepers can protect the castle and keep out destructive hordes. But they also exclude others from the treasure inside. With the massive increase of information, a desire for convenience, and our distrust for these gatekeepers, algorithms have become the new castle walls. And just like with their human builders, algorithms are faulty.

Some of the faults of algorithms include:

- Inscrutability: Unlike a human, there's often not a default system for recourse when an algorithm denies you a job or loan.

- Bias: Algorithms learn from associations between common words. Humans learn this way too, and those associations can lead to stereotypes, generalizations, and harmful ideas about groups of people. Both humans and algorithms have biases, but humans are more likely to be aware of their biases.

- Lack of accountability: Algorithms, with their secretive and protected content, are not subject to regulation and checks and balances. Developers should evaluate these algorithms, and many do, but often algorithms run untested and unchallenged.

- Engagement issues: Algorithms are designed to get people to engage and stay on a platform or product as long as possible. This can affect users' mental health and make it harder for them to stay away from the screen.

- Extremism: Algorithms reinforce the negative and stronger feelings. Social media was and is designed to get attention: likes, comments, shares, retweets. Negativity often flows to the top of social media feeds because of this process and can affect the user (Nead, 2020).

Media literacy and digital citizenship must educate users on algorithms and their pluses and minuses. Algorithms don't just control our flow of information but also who gets credit or a job; they drive our cars and run our plants. They are embedded in all parts of our lives, but we don't notice and often don't understand them.

More importantly, algorithms define "truth" to the user. People rarely look beyond the first page of a Google search. They often believe the first result delivered by the algorithm is the truth. Many times, it is. If you are asking Google, "What is Newton's Second Law of Motion?" you'll get the correct answer every time. But if you ask Google, "Why did the Roman Empire fall?" you're going to get a variety of answers, each with different evidence, opinions, and sometimes bias. When we delegate part of critical thinking to algorithms, we risk being misdirected, misinformed, and missing facts.

Other technology trends reinforce these powerful algorithms. The CO-VID-19 pandemic increased the use of the already-growing trend of smart speakers (Richter, 2020). A 2020 study by Edison Research and NPR found that as many as 35 percent of Americans during the pandemic are "consuming more news and information through such devices" (Daws, 2020). In 2022 smart speaker ownership in the United States was 35%, with Amazon having the most popular products (Lebow, 2022). When Amazon introduced the Amazon Echo and Alexa in 2014, it was an immediate success, with more companies introducing such devices. These speakers are convenient, and many use them to listen to music or podcasts. But they're also used for answering questions and finding information. Unlike the Google search engine, a smart speaker is only going to deliver one response. You can't see the options of answers like on a web page. Even less thought and evaluation occur when you are literally told the one and only answer. Like with Google search, the answer is often correct, but not always. As more children grow up in homes with smart speakers, with information at their fingertips or with a word, they grow even more accustomed to outsourcing their information seeking and "truth" to devices. Younger generations may have even less experience finding information in this digital environment, which is another reason media literacy is so important.

How can educators teach media literacy in this tech-saturated, algorithmic world? Along with using the updated media literacy standards with AASL and Common Core, librarians should update the traditional way that media literacy is taught. You may remember learning about the 5Ws—Who, What Where, When, and Why—for evaluating information. Perhaps you were given an article and then asked to fill out a worksheet, or the teacher asked the class to identify what was being said and why. These 5Ws are important; they ground the student in a process of inquiry and educate on how to be skeptical of media.

Librarians, teachers, and media specialists should update how they teach the 5Ws. Trends in technology have outpaced instructional trends (Rogers-Whitehead, 2020). *How* we find information has changed over the last generation. Here are some suggestions to adapt the 5Ws for the 21st century and under the subject of digital citizenship.

- **Who?** During the 2020 presidential election, researchers from Carnegie Mellon University found about two times as much bot activity as human activity online. From their research, they discovered that from January 2020 through the election "82 percent of the top 50 influential retweeters are bots." These bots were 20 percent of all tweets involving political conspiracy theories like QAnon (Metz, 2020). As Twitter and other social media platforms crack down on these bots or automated software, the accounts become more sophisticated and harder to detect. When instructing on the Who of a media source, librarians should realize that "Who" is not necessarily an actual person.

- **What?** Social media algorithms are driven by engagement, not reality. This means posts and comments that drive emotions filter up to the top of feeds and are more widely shared. With this controversial algorithmic reality, a crucial part of media literacy is evaluating not other media, but ourselves. Users should be more aware of their emotional responses to the media.

- **Where?** As discussed before, finding information on a smart speaker is different than on a search engine. Mobile devices also change our search and reading habits. The smaller screen makes it harder to dive into deeper content, and people on mobile devices are more likely to use the voice assistants and the smart searching enabled there. The "Where" can also be the browser used. A browser that tracks searches and uses cookies may bring back different results than a private browser.

- **When?** Journalists and media outlets are pressured more than ever before to churn out stories fast. The 24/7 newsroom and people's appetite for information make speed sometimes more of a priority than accuracy. Sometimes misinformation spreads from the first media outlet out of the gate, missing a fact—and that falsehood rapidly spreads from other outlets picking up the story. Outlets that update their stories regularly, print their errors, and acknowledge that the story is "developing" can be trusted more than others.

- **Why?** The last W, "Why," asks about the motivations of the message. But with websites and social media, sometimes this "Why" is even more difficult to follow. Domain names are not very regulated, and websites don't always include an author or even a date posted. It can be unclear who or what funds a website or organization (Rogers-Whitehead, 2020).

As we teach students how to evaluate information in the 21st century, a good start is by reevaluating how we teach them to evaluate. The rules of the game have shifted, and there are more players than ever in our media ecosystem. We are all those players as well—sharing our own content in our own smaller ecosystems. Teaching an updated 5Ws helps us, the players, to better navigate the game.

Media Literacy Programming in the Library

Curtis Rogers is the director of communications with the Urban Library Council, and he feels the United States has experienced a "huge wakeup call" recently. "The events that happened in the Capitol at the beginning of the year have served as a wake-up call and a conversation starter to look at how massively powerful the information technologies we use are for in sustaining or putting in danger our shared democracy. Libraries have always been engines of democracy." Libraries are that third space, a place for all classes, abilities, races, and genders to converge together. They can also be that community gathering space for understanding, talking across dividing lines, and healing. But for that to happen, libraries need to have consensus and self-reflection on what their goals and practices are in media literacy.

As described earlier, media literacy, like digital citizenship, is a broad term that encompasses multiple skills and overlapping standards. We already have our echo systems and opinions on what "news" is, and that can affect how we create programs around it. Many factors are involved in media literacy, and it can be easy to just focus on one element while leaving out the rest. Rogers calls for an "intentional focus of conversation" on the subject, but acknowledges not all libraries are on the same page. "A lot of time when there are news literacy and media literacy programs a lot of the conversations are on traditional news, but it's not necessarily spreading the same way."

Librarians are working adults and most likely don't have the same experiences online as younger people. They use different communication tools, speak differently online, and may not be familiar with newer social media and platforms. There's always a generational gap with technology. At one time, radio was the new-fangled invention the older generation couldn't wrap their head around. This gap in knowledge and experience is nothing new, but part of providing high-quality media literacy education to younger people is an attempt to listen to their experiences and incorporate them in any programming.

Rogers recommends librarians try to get on the same page. "There needs to be some knowledge building and some exploration of best practices and what are effective solutions." Some of those best practices can be found in the organizations described in this chapter or through using Common Core or AASL standards. Others can be built through that self-reflection. When creating a media literacy program, library staff can ask themselves:

- What is my purpose in creating this program?

- What type of media am I focused on?

- Who is my audience? Is my audience utilizing that type of media?

- What type of media do I use? Are there media/platforms out there I'm unfamiliar with?

- How do I define what a reputable source is?

- What types of paid and vetted resources do the libraries have that I can share? Do I know how to use those resources?

- How will I handle questions/comments of those in the program that may disagree with what I am saying about the media?

Librarians should be prepared for pushback. The area of media literacy can be political. Describing someone's source of news as not reputable or full of conspiracy theories may cause them to take offense and push back. Making broad generalizations about any media can bring up "whataboutisms" and make the audience less receptive. While there are certainly better sources than others, oftentimes even highly partisan media has a grain of truth or fact in it. Conspiracy theories are often built around one fact that got twisted and misinterpreted. For example, with QAnon, while the conspiracy may have greatly exaggerated and misled followers about incidents of pedophilia in the government and high places, child sexual abuse and trafficking is a real thing.

"One of the tricky things about media literacy is that nobody is immune to it," Rogers said. We all have our own biases and information silos. He recommends listening, collaborating, and talking to others as you build your library programs. "For example, we had a library who was working with a school on a project where the youth were researching something and there were no guidelines around it, like what a good database you can use is. Being able to provide that type of framework or protocol to say, 'hey we have something on hand at the library' helps libraries to say, 'this is why it's important not to just have people rely on Google'" (Urban Libraries Council, n.d.).

More public libraries are offering media literacy programs. After the 2016 U.S. presidential election and the trending of the words "fake news," more libraries offered this type of programming. For example, local libraries in Cook County in Chicago offered media literacy in 2017 and beyond. As reported in the *Chicago Tribune*, one library, Highland Park, hosted "several media literacy forums dubbed 'Consider the source: Not all information is created equal.'" In that program, library staff helped attendees know the tools, databases, and other strategies for fact-checking information and for more help with digital literacy (Gaines, 2019). Libraries, with their paid and peer-reviewed databases, can show the basics of searching through engines other than Google. They can also show other search techniques and browsers that patrons may not have used.

Another Chicago-area library, Lake Forest, is dealing with another issue related to media literacy: having conversations around challenging conversation topics. They previously hosted panels called "Common Ground Conversations" (Gaines, 2019). Libraries, being a neutral, nonpartisan area open for all, can be an ideal space for tough discussions.

An alternative way to help educate on media literacy through a digital citizenship lens is through encouraging lateral reading. Lateral reading is the process of looking at multiple sources on the same topic to better evaluate the content and bias. A sample program for lateral reading can be found in Appendix A.

Questions to Ask to Teach and Encourage Media Literacy

Librarians curate booklists, pathfinders, and more content to help their patrons and students. Media literacy pathfinders, posters, and visual information can help. By putting questions and pamphlets near computers and checkouts, the librarian can both passively and actively encourage a deeper inquiry into one's consumption of media. Here are some question prompts to educate students or to create materials of your own to share:

1. Does going online change your feelings? Or does it just reinforce them?

2. How did the person posting/sharing this content get their information? Did they cite things? How did they conduct their research?

3. Do you need information from a certain part of the world? Are you only looking at sources that may be in a specific region?

4. Does the media report primary research? If so, do they document that, and what's the research?

5. Are facts or opinions being offered?

There are more questions to ask when evaluating media through the 5Ws. Rather than simply ask "Who" or "Why," students should dig in deeper. Here are some suggested questions to ask:

- Who? Was this a human or bot who created this?
    - When did this person join the platform?
    - How much do they post?
    - Who do they retweet/share, etc.?
- What? What am I feeling about what the media is saying?
    - What emotional state am I in when consuming this content?
    - After consuming this content, what do I want to do?
- Where? Where am I accessing my information?
    - What is the best way to search for this information? A smart speaker? Phone? Desktop PC?
    - How many answers do I want from this research? Am I simply wanting one answer, or am I evaluating different sides of an issue?
    - What search engine am I using to look for information? Have I cleared out my cookies and cache on that search engine?
- When? When did this article/post come out?
    - Is there an update to this story?
    - When did this story originally come out?
    - How old are the sources this story cites?
- Why? Why is this message being created and shared?
    - Who is the author, owner, and funder of the site?
    - What advertisements are on the site?
    - What does this site link to?

Digital Law and Digital Rights and Responsibilities

What Are Digital Rights and Responsibilities?

In the aftermath of the January 6 Capitol attack, many conversations emerged. These conversations and controversies continue. Some were related to media literacy: How did the people there believe such conspiracy theories? What are the effects of these media echo chambers? But other conversations centered around digital law and digital rights and responsibilities. Amazon decided to deplatform the right-wing social media app Parler after its connections to the Capitol insurrection. Google and Apple app stores also removed the app. Donald Trump was impeached for inciting the Capitol insurrection, and part of the process was a debate around free speech. Thousands of groups, profiles, and accounts have been removed from Facebook, Twitter, YouTube, and other platforms in the wake of the attack (Fung, 2021). These debates and discourse have brought renewed questions around what exactly people's digital rights and responsibilities are and what is the reach of digital law. Librarians play a key role in educating on these topics.

The concepts of digital law and digital rights and responsibilities are included in Dr. Mike Ribble's nine elements of digital citizenship (Ribble, 2015). But what are they exactly? Professor RonNell Anderson Jones is the Lee E. Teitelbaum Endowed Professor of Law at the University of Utah. She regularly researches and speaks on media, transparency, and emerging areas of social media law. Jones describes digital rights and responsibilities:

> In many respects, our digital rights and responsibilities are parallel to the rights and responsibilities that we have in the offline world. The trick is learning how to translate the components of good citizenship, healthy interaction, necessary legal obligation, and meaningful education into this new space—with an eye toward both its distinctive advantages and its unique risks. There are a lot of complex balances we have always had to strike on questions of free speech and harm—for example, balancing between the right to express oneself and the need to protect individuals from harmful speech, or between the desire to share materials and the need to protect creators' property rights—and all of these tensions continue to exist in the digital space. We are learning that many of these tensions are amplified in new ways by the changing media environment.

The fallout after the January 6 Capitol riot highlights these tensions Jones speaks of. Twitter permanently banned former President Donald Trump on January 8, 2021, stating, "After close review of recent Tweets from the @realDonaldTrump account and the context around them we have permanently suspended the account due to the risk of further incitement of violence" (Fung, 2019). This action produced cheers and anxieties. It also brought up concerns around the power of tech companies like Twitter and what speech should be protected. Former German Chancellor Angela Merkel expressed concern about Twitter's decision and those of other social media companies, describing them as "problematic." Her spokesman Steffen Seibert said of Merkel's response, "This fundamental right can be intervened in, but according to the law and within the framework defined by legislators—not according to a decision by the management of social media platforms" (Lemon, 2021). Seibert and others see the role of government as determining free speech. But as so much of our speech is made online and within the walled gardens of social media platforms, it's beyond the reach of the government to intervene. The interaction between the press and government, social media, and institutions is another concept around digital rights and responsibilities.

Jones also adds that "when we speak about digital rights and responsibilities, we mean that we will think carefully about not only the laws that bind us, but also the norms that guide us, both as speakers and as listeners. A community of speakers always has a set of expectations and obligations, and this is as true when we are posting, commenting, emailing, or sharing online as it is when we are communicating in other spaces." Librarians have a role in helping students determine those norms and creating their norms in library spaces. More about how librarians can help amplify speech and help others self-advocate will be discussed in Chapter 4.

What Is Digital Law?

Another part of digital citizenship is a basic understanding of digital law. This is a broad, changing, and growing area. Jones describes it as follows:

> Almost any subarea of law might find itself veering into the area of "digital law" when questions arise about the way that old legal rules map onto new online situations. In wide swaths of American jurisprudence—from contract law to free speech law to corporate law to intellectual property law—we have had to tussle with the new realities of our increasingly digital world.

Even family and criminal law interact with what can be termed digital law. Our digital footprints can affect us in legal decisions; digital evidence can be its smoking gun. A big part of digital law that intersects information science is intellectual property. These laws protect the ownership of ideas, literary and artistic works, and inventions. Young people should understand these basic laws because they affect their online lives. A sample program for teaching copyright law is in Appendix B. Definitions under intellectual property law include:

- **Patents:** These are granted by the U.S. government and give the patent owner the exclusive right to an invention for 14 or 20 years. Patents include processes, designs, machines, and even living organisms like plants.

- **Trademarks:** These are the names, words, symbols, or devices that identify and distinguish a good or service. Trademarks have great financial value and are often referred to as brand names.

- **Copyright:** A copyright is a legal protection given to the creator of a work. These creative works include books, movies, photographs, art, music, and more.

- **Trade secrets:** This refers to information kept confidential to provide a competitive advantage. Trade secrets are not protected by federal law, but they are protected by the states. Examples of trade secrets may be the recipe for Kentucky Fried Chicken or the formula for Pepsi (Solomon et al., 2016).

Intellectual property law in the United States was created long before digital media. The laws around copyright were created with different creative works in mind. In 1998 the federal government attempted to rectify that with the Digital Millennium Copyright Act (DCMA) that protects digital copyrighted material from unauthorized use. Within the DMCA there is a law called Safe Harbor. This law carves out protections for websites that passively host user content. This means sites like YouTube and TikTok are not liable for any copyright infringement of their users. The Safe Harbor law also applies to trademarks, patents, and foreign copyrighted material. Without the DMCA, the Internet would look very different. These large platforms, like Steam, Instagram, etc., would not exist. The DMCA makes these sites platforms, not publishers (Kalia & McSherry, 2015). There is continuing debate over these protections. Jones said, "The ease with which intellectual property can be copied and shared creates a heightened need for citizens to have some knowledge of the contours of copyright law. The wider point here is that in addition to setting *social and cultural* expectations about our rights and responsibilities in the digital space, we also are setting the *legal* expectations that we will have in these areas."

Digital law also affects online privacy. What can users consent to? What is allowed to be tracked, gathered, and/or sold? Digital law affects all of us, every day. If you've downloaded an app, you've signed a legal agreement. "The digital world puts most people in a position of having to read and accept terms and conditions of use for the apps that they download—an interaction with contract law that people a generation ago might not have had," said Jones. "The many moments of online activity in which platforms, search engines, or websites are gathering private information and tracking data about a specific user mean that privacy law is taking shape in new ways for ordinary people." Online privacy will be discussed more in Chapter 3.

Digital Law and the Economy

Digital law also affects our ability to engage with the global online economy. Individuals, particularly young people, have an opportunity to reach other markets, people, ideas, and more than ever before. But this opportunity also comes with risks. Being more connected and with our livelihoods so intertwined with technology, we become vulnerable to a platform's policy changes, or it completely disappears.

On June 29, 2020, about 600 million people lost access to the app TikTok. People in India loved TikTok; at the time around 44 percent of them used it, making income, mobilizing protests, and of course, as entertainment. The Indian government did not like TikTok, and as of this writing, the app is still banned in the country. The ban came from clashes with China, which owns ByteDance, the company that owns TikTok. There are land disputes along the Chinese and Indian border, and the two countries have long-standing conflicts. After banning the app, India has been pushing their domestic apps, but so far there hasn't been one app that's filled the void, although many scams and fake apps have sprouted (Pahwa, 2020).

What does it mean when an entire country bans an app? What happens to the users? The content? There were ethical concerns about TikTok with some of its content and cybersecurity flaws. But there are also ethical concerns about inhibiting free speech in the name of protectionism and one entity making unliteral decisions for hundreds of millions. What does it mean when the government steps in to regulate technology? What happens when they don't? Who, if anyone, should be the one to ban and regulate apps? These are big questions that aren't going away.

Harvard's Berkman Klein Center for Internet and Society put out a report in 2020 on youth and the digital economy. In it, they described some of the "new asymmetries" in the digital economy.

Consider, for instance, social media platforms, online video services, instant messaging systems, and games that are tremendously popular among youth. Most of these platforms and services are commercial spaces with advertising-based revenue models. This means that they provide "free" services on which youth can socialize, communicate, learn, and play. In return, however, youth indirectly pay for these services by being the recipients of targeted ads. In order to be able to better target these ads, the platforms and services collect, aggregated, and analyze the massive amounts of data youth generate about themselves. (Lombana et al., 2020)

Young people, in particular, may even be less aware of the extent to which their data is shared. And they may not understand the digital law around these online contracts and agreements they agree to. The Youth and the Digital Economy Report describes young people, and all of us really, as "prosumers" (Lombana et al., 2020). We are producing content on platforms, whether that be our words, art, sounds, or more. But we are also consuming other people's content in the same places. The platforms on which we produce and consume this content hold vast amounts of power. The role of digital citizenship education is educating about the roles of platforms and publishers in all of our lives and how we as "prosumers" can better understand our rights and the law.

There's also a misunderstanding about these social media policies and our ability to freely participate in them, whether in an economic way or just to communicate. Jones said,

> The social media platform that hosts your speech is making content-moderation decisions that determine what the speech environment that you occupy will feel like. These are found in the terms and conditions that you agree to at the time you sign up for an account. It would be helpful if citizens understood the power that is held by major platforms. If they thought more carefully about the power they have as consumers to decide where they engage in speech.

Young people do not know a time in their lives without social media. They don't necessarily have the same expectations of privacy as older generations. They may see technology as ubiquitous and inevitable and be less concerned about commercial data practices. In smaller classroom surveys I have conducted with adolescents through Digital Respons-Ability, I have found this. They think less about privacy than I assumed. These conversations and surveys with teens have been backed up with larger national surveys, such as a 2019 survey with Common Sense Media that found that in some contexts teens are less concerned about some social media platforms' business and privacy models (Common Sense Media, 2019).

This generational gap is a space where librarians and other adults can teach about the systemic laws, responsibilities, policies, platforms, and politics that are all around the Internet. Librarians can help young people protect their content and creativity through digital law.

The Youth in the Digital Economy Report summarizes this tension of the Internet: "On the one hand, youth are empowered by the digital ecosystem because they are provided with the tools and spaces to exercise their agency as active and creative consumers and producers of culture. At the same time, corporate platforms commodify their data, attention, culture, labor, and creativity for profits that are not equitably shared" (Lombana et al., 2020).

The Capitol Riots of January 6 were a wake-up call to many. They brought attention to divisive, partisan politics and the importance of democracy but also to our media and digital ecosystems. The importance of understanding these systems is critical. Librarians have a vital role in planning the conversations and education needed to wake up more of us. "Understanding digital rights and responsibilities and digital law are important because communication in digital spaces—email, apps, social media—is now ubiquitous," said Jones. "The online world is central to who we are and how we communicate, and this makes an appreciation for how that world operates critically important." Media literacy—how we share, evaluate, and view communications—frames our interactions in the online world and in person. Media literacy affects our democracy.

Jones continues, "Every strong democracy needs thoughtful, clear, useful communication on matters of public concern. It needs trustworthy information, shared factual truth, social connectivity, and constructive debate on issues of importance. An understanding of digital rights and responsibilities is central to civic education because, without it, we cannot have the conversations that sustain a system of self-government and a prosperous, healthy community." Libraries create community, and for communities to prosper and come together, conversations—often difficult ones—are needed.

The mission of libraries—to freely share information—requires a healthy democracy. And a healthy democracy needs shared truth, connections, and conversation. Teaching and advocating for digital citizenship, such as educating on media literacy, digital law, and digital rights and responsibilities, is a core part of librarianship.

CHAPTER 2

Communication and Etiquette

I regularly teach parents how to navigate technology with their children. In these presentations, the parents are surveyed about what they feel are the biggest impacts of technology on their family. A top concern I've found with parents is that they feel their children are not communicative. They see their children frequently on a phone or other device. That's a legitimate complaint. Having children engage socially with the world around them is a vital developmental skill. However, I would argue that young people *are* communicative, maybe more so than any other generation. They are just communicating differently. Older generations would frequently communicate in person or on a shared phone call. Their spaces were more public, around adults, and out loud. Younger generations are communicating more privately and quietly in text-based conversations and in places where adults are not listening.

Social media usage statistics compiled from the review site Tech Injury reported in 2021 that 350 million photos are uploaded to Facebook every day. Also, in 24 hours there are about 500 million tweets and over 300 billion emails sent (Bulao, 2021). The data analytics company Domo narrows down the data even further with its annual "Data Never Sleeps" report. They found that the average person spent twice as much time on streaming services in 2021 than 2020. The report also shared that TikTok users watched 167 million videos every minute (Hathaway, 2021). These numbers are most likely higher in 2021, in part because of the pandemic and will grow in 2022. People are communicating constantly. The quantity of communication has increased, but not necessarily the quality. What has changed in communication is the platform and the context.

This chapter will explore two vital elements of digital citizenship: digital communication and digital etiquette. It will also discuss ways librarians can teach and advocate around the rapidly evolving world of digital communications. We are speaking more than ever before, but across different platforms, devices, and with different company policies. Libraries, always bastions of free speech and accessible information, are essential places for education, advocacy, and more about communication.

Standards and Definitions of Digital Communication and Digital Etiquette

Simply put, digital communication is exchanging data in digital form. The data can be code, symbols, words, or numbers; the data is unorganized and random. Computers take that code or symbols and turn them into information. We take that information and give it meaning. That last step, interpreting the information into some kind of significance, is the most complicated. A host of factors help us derive meaning from information, such as:

- Past experiences

- Culture

- Race and ethnicity

- Language

- The delivery mechanism of the information

- Biological factors such as tiredness, pain, or hunger

- Our emotional state

- The context where the information was received

- Who delivered the information

Complicating that last step of interpretation further is the lack of nonverbal and physical cues in digital communication. In the 1960s Professor Mehrabian created a model on how messages sent with nonverbal cues were interpreted. He found that only 7 percent of messages were interpreted based on what the actual words spoken meant. From that research, Mehrabian found that facial expression communicated the most—not gestures, not the words itself, but what the face looked like when communicating (Mehrabian & Weiner, 1967). While digital communication may use emoji faces or GIFs, it's not the same as facial expression. Strategies for with the very complicated nature of sending and receiving the info..... will be discussed later in this chapter.

Digital etiquette, sometimes referred to as netiquette, is defined by digital citizenship scholar Mike Ribble as "the standards of conduct expected by other digital technology users." To be a participating digital citizen, one should be aware of norms and standards of behavior online. These norms and standards can shift wildly depending on the platform, device, and type of communication. While there are some agreed-upon standards in digital etiquette in public forms and when writing an email, social media is trickier. Librarians and other educators can assist young people with deciphering this shifting landscape of standards, policies, and behaviors.

What are the standards around digital citizenship and digital communication? The American Association of School Librarians (AASL) describes learner, or student, competencies when participating with global learning communities. The standards state that learners should interact with others of differing perspectives. The AASL standards also encourage learners to engage "in informed conversation and active debate" and contribute "to discussions in which multiple viewpoints on a topic are expressed." AASL also has a shared foundation of collaboration to "work effectively with others to broaden perspectives and work toward common goals." To assist collaboration, the standards encourage learners to "use a variety of communication tools and resources" and establish "connections with other learners to build on their prior knowledge and create new knowledge" (AASL, 2021).

This global mindset of communication and collaboration can also be found in the ISTE student standards. One of the seven standards for students is "global collaborator," where "students use digital tools to broaden their perspectives and enrich their learning by collaborating with others and working effectively in teams locally and globally" (ISTE, n.d.). Students have the opportunity to communicate faster and more globally than ever before. In an instant, they can be talking to individuals of different ages, cultures, countries, and past experiences. A digital citizen has a global mindset, an understanding of the world, and its place in it. Digital communication is that passport for global digital citizens.

Another ISTE standard for students is "creative communicator," where "students communicate clearly and express themselves creatively for a variety of purposes using the platforms, tools, styles, formats and digital media appropriate to their goals" (ISTE, n.d.). Converting information we receive online is difficult. Being the transmitter of that information can be even harder. The ability to "clearly" express information online, stripped of tone and gestures, is a heavy lift, but a necessary one. Part of that difficulty is the variety of "platforms, tools, styles, formats and digital media" online (ISTE, n.d.). There is a bewildering forest of groups, forums, boards, apps, and channels, all with their digital etiquette. Yet we must learn to traverse that path. Being able to communicate on various channels is vital work and a personal skill. If someone cannot properly communicate, they can be shut off not just from work, commerce, and education but also from connection. Platforms and communication tools not only have digital etiquette standards but culture. What are those microcultures? How can travelers from different platforms understand them? How can librarians understand the digital culture and share that understanding with students and patrons?

Digital Culture

You've traveled to a new land and are feeling bewildered. The natives are speaking a different language; you can pick out some of the words but aren't quite grasping the meaning. You brought a map you used in your own country, but it's not helping you navigate here. You try to reach out to some locals but they ignore you or even laugh at you. Around you, people are wearing different outfits with odd slogans and logos. You try to find a friendly guide, but since your map doesn't work, you just keep wandering around. You ask yourself, "What am I doing here? Why did I leave Facebook for this place?"

The Internet is full of different lands, countries, customs, and rules. If you are an avid Facebook user and then jump to Reddit, a very different social media platform, you may feel bewildered. Reddit is built around anonymity and is less image and video based. On Facebook, your name and face follow you around the platform. Even within platforms, there are varying rules. A Facebook group may have strict or less strict moderation. Every group, or subreddit, on Reddit, has its own rules and moderators. All of these groups and platforms have their communication. There are popular GIFs, slang, in-jokes, memes, hashtags, mascots, and more spread across groups and forums online. Even if you speak the language in that forum, you may not speak the dialect.

New languages are being built as we speak on these platforms. And those languages are not always words. The Library of Congress recognizes this and now archives memes; they have preserved sites like Know Your Meme and Urban Dictionary. Gretchen McCulloch is a linguist and the author of *Because Internet: Understanding the New Rules of Language*. She describes language as "humanity's most spectacular open-source project" (McCulloch, 2020). With the Internet and more humans involved, this creation of language has sped up. She calls out Twitter as a big source of this. "It's not an accident that Twitter, where you're encouraged to follow people you don't already know, has given rise to more linguistic innovation (not to mention memes and social movements) than Facebook, where you primarily friend people you already know offline" (McCulloch, 2020). Traveling in these foreign digital spaces with strangers can be bewildering, but it also pushes us to new ideas, new cultures, and new languages.

Are we preparing young people to communicate in these different languages and cultures? Do they have transferable communication skills? Can they listen and learn from other spaces? Can they still follow digital etiquette even though that etiquette may vary from place to place? Teaching students the context of language teaches them communication. There are certain things you say and do *not* say in different places. In real life, you would not shout at a funeral. And there are digital spaces where SHOUTING IN ALL CAPS is not appropriate either. We need to not only help guide people on *what* to say but *where* to say it.

An activity a librarian can try with students is giving them prompts and scenarios for tasks. Then the students must answer what is the best social media platform for those tasks and explain why.

Some questions to help students think about the "where" include:

- How would you stay in contact with your grandma?

- Where would you find help with homework?

- Where would you show pictures of your vacation?

- Where do you go for news?

- How would you learn what hairstyle works best for you?

- Where would you look to find a job?

There is no right or wrong answer to these questions; it's more like "good" or "best." By thinking about culture and context, young people can better communicate and be heard.

Multilingual Digital Communication

The International Computer and Information Literacy Study assess the information and communications technology of teachers and students. Its latest international survey was released in 2019 and tested students' computer and information literacy skills. Students internally averaged about 496 on a scale from 100 to 700. Officials with the study said that students don't "develop sophisticated digital skills" just because they've grown up with devices. The organization's executive director, Dirk Hastedt, said in a statement, "It's essential that young people are taught these skills at schools, and that their teachers are well supported in delivering this bedrock of modern education" (Jacobson, 2019).

Assuming young people know how to *use* devices just because they *have* devices is something parents, teachers, and other adults may believe. But data doesn't support that. Other results from the survey found that in the United States, "8th graders can use computers to gather basic information and make simple edits. They have some awareness of security risks in the digital world. But they're less likely to understand the purpose of sponsored content on a website, use generic mapping software or know how to control color and text when creating a presentation." Overall, middle school students' tech skills are "low-to-medium" (Jacobson, 2019).

Part of those tech skills includes being able to transfer knowledge from one device or software to another. Twenty-first-century workers need to work with multiple types of software, on mobile and desktop devices, with different operating systems and different user interfaces. During the COVID-19 pandemic, many office workers had to learn fast how to use multiple web conferencing software platforms. Digital literacy skills can't just be on one device or one interface; they have to be on all of them.

Students must be multilingual not only on the varying platforms of different cultures but with different digital ecosystems and operating systems. They need to know how to complete the same tasks on a mobile device and a desktop, iOS, and Android. Hardware and operating systems have culture too. For example, there is a robust, and somewhat obsessive, culture around Apple products. Apple has a different brand and feel and recently has united behind their privacy controls. They pride themselves on exclusivity and price, while Android works to reach a broader audience. Android has more apps and lower costs. With both operating systems and products there are different names, icons, and shortcuts. Just like navigating different social media platforms, navigating different hardware platforms is an important digital citizenship skill.

Communication and Context

Written communication, unlike in-person communication, is stripped of context. When we converse with others, they can hear our tone and the pacing in our message. They can see our facial expressions, eyebrows raised, eye contact, mouth twisting in different directions, and all the other tiny movements. This type of communication is rich with meaning but lacking in speed, memory, and efficiency. There is no one perfect type of communication. Emails can spread messages widely but lack nonverbal cues.

A podcast can transmit the tone of the message but is more ephemeral and harder to search through. Social media can reach a huge audience but can also be misinterpreted by that audience. Good communicators and digital citizens recognize both the benefits and flaws in different types of communication and adjust their approach depending on the audience and context.

Beyond understanding the culture of the different communication platforms, digital citizens must contextualize the content. This means adjusting the message of the words to the audience. This is something marketers do constantly. A company trying to sell a product must understand their market—the demographics, their preferences, their habits, and their platforms. While most of us aren't selling a product online, we are still selling something. We may be trying to get buy-in for an idea, or attention, or trying to advocate for a cause we care about.

That concept of attention is something that advertisers, educators, economists, and all of us are concerned with online. Research from many disciplines says that humans have limited cognitive resources and can only give so much attention. Therefore, attention is a scarce resource and very valuable. Psychologist and economist Herbert A. Simon wrote about this concept in the 1970s, "In an information-rich world, the wealth of information means a dearth of something else: a scarcity of whatever it is that information consumes. What information consumes is rather obvious: it consumes the attention of its recipients" (Simon, 1971). We all are competing in this attention economy and must take care that our audience hears us.

But who is the audience? That depends on the message. With in-person communication, speakers must "read the room." I remember doing this a lot when I was a youth services librarian running storytimes for toddlers and preschoolers. Young children have even less attention to give. I would need to closely watch the crowd. Were they watching me? Were they sitting, or had they stood up to wander around the room? Were they participating with their words and gestures? Were the parents watching or looking at their phones? One hundred percent attention from young children is impossible, but I'd try to aim for over half! If that started dipping, I'd have to decide about my communication. Was this book not age-appropriate? Was I not reading with enough energy and enthusiasm? Or was today just a bad day for everyone?

It's exponentially more difficult to read the room online, but there are strategies we can employ. First, you can break your audience into formal versus informal. Preschoolers are an informal audience; you shouldn't use big words, they're not your boss (although they may feel that way sometimes!). With informal communication, there's more flexibility, more room for slang and jokes, a space for memes, GIFs, and emojis. Contrast this with formal communication. An example of formal communication may be from a student to a professor. Formal communication is more common in work environments. You have to be very careful about joking on company email. If you are talking to a grandparent, you may use more formal communication because their generation has a different culture around how younger people talk to elders. Formal versus informal communication is also influenced by culture. For example, if you were raised in the Deep South of the United States, you may be more likely to use "ma'am" or "sir" when speaking.

After deciding whether you need to employ more formal or informal communication, consider whether the information needs to be public or private. Digital citizens should assume that information shared online is never 100 percent private, although there are certain platforms and means to make it more discreet. If you are trying to reach a large audience, like a PR professional sharing a press release, or you have a big announcement to make, then go public. Use a platform where the information can be seen by everyone. If you are sharing something more intimate, controversial, related to only a few people, or just random thoughts, perhaps choose a different platform or means of communication.

Deciding if the information you want to share is public or private also helps you stay safer online. Here's a basic table of some information that can be shared publicly (and often is, without your permission) versus other information you should try to keep private.

What information should be public or private online?

Public Information	Private Information
Name (some sites require this; others just want a username)	Location
Public profile picture	Other pictures of yourself
Username	Your contacts
Bio (some sites require this, others do not; if it is required, keep it short and vague)	Interests, hobbies, saved links, and videos
Public IP address (aka Internet IP)	Financial information
Email address (almost always needed for an account)	Phone number (not always required for an account)

Finally, when deciding how best to craft and share your message, ask yourself, should this be shared in person or online? Despite its conveniences and efficiency, communicating online may not be the best in certain

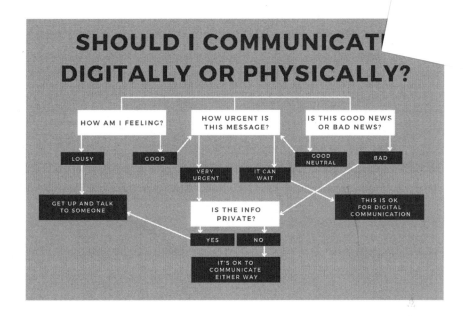

SHOULD I COMMUNICAT[E] DIGITALLY OR PHYSICALLY?

HOW AM I FEELING? — LOUSY → GET UP AND TALK TO SOMEONE — GOOD

HOW URGENT IS THIS MESSAGE? — VERY URGENT — IT CAN WAIT

IS THIS GOOD NEWS OR BAD NEWS? — GOOD NEUTRAL — BAD

IS THE INFO PRIVATE? — YES — NO

THIS IS OK FOR DIGITAL COMMUNICATION

IT'S OK TO COMMUNICATE EITHER WAY

circumstances. Here's a chart to help you decide whether to share the message in person or online.

Public versus private, informal versus formal, online versus in person: these are all questions and decisions digital citizens need to make when deciding how, what, and where to communicate. Communication is complicated enough, but stripped of its context, digital communication can be even harder. Young people need to be taught skills around digital communication. It's not enough to be told what to say; they need to be taught how and where to say it. Being a digital citizen is about learning the skills to navigate the online world. Some of the skills important to digitally communicate include:

- Self-awareness: Understanding your goal and motivations for communication, knowing your emotions at the time of communication

- Empathy: Understanding the potential effects of your communication on your audience, grasping where your audience is online, interpreting others' information online with the best intent

- Critical thinking: Evaluating your messages online and crafting them in a way to reach your goals

Librarians can help model and mentor digital communication and encourage its practice. You can't get better at writing if you don't write. And you can't get better at digital communication unless you do it. Communication is a lifelong practice, and we can use guides along the way.

Freedom of Speech and Digital Law

After the Capitol insurrection on January 6, the social media network Parler was banned from Apple and Google stores, making it inaccessible to almost all smartphone users. Amazon also refused to host the site anymore, effectively taking it off the Internet. The app was removed because both companies said that it was violating their rules against harmful content. The app, which advertises itself as a place for free speech, did make changes for Apple, and, as of May 17, 2021, was back on the App Store. Parler is still suspended indefinitely on Amazon and uses a different hosting provider now. It's also not on Google Play as of this writing (Bond, 2021).

The de-platforming of Parler, coming at the same time as former President Donald Trump was banned from Twitter and other social media accounts, has put more fire into the debate around free speech online. It's also brought up important discussions of the power of big tech. How much power do these companies have? And are we comfortable with that? These are big questions that Internet users will be grappling with for a long time.

As social media companies have used more moderating tools and banned, removed, and made other changes, other questions have been brought up around what free speech is. In recent years, as discussions around #MeToo and other movements have demanded more accountability, the words "canceling" or "cancel culture" have grown in usage. The reactions from some corners of the Internet about Parler losing its platform used those terms. Writers, politicians, and others have pressed for legislative change in reaction to situations like Parler. Merriam-Webster Dictionary even added new definitions of "canceled" or "cancel culture" in January 2021 (Merriam-Webster, n.d.).

What does the law say about free speech? And what are the potential implications of big tech "canceling" accounts and users? What do we as digital citizens need to know about free speech online? RonNell Andersen Jones is the Lee E. Teitelbaum Endowed Professor of Law at the University of Utah. She researches legal issues around social media law and the role of the courts with media. When asked what she thought people should understand from these discussions of de-platforming and "cancel culture," Jones responded:

> . . . It would be helpful for people to better understand the basics contours of constitutional doctrine. There is significant confusion about what the First Amendment requires in these situations. When Twitter decides not to let someone speak on its platform, this is a decision by a private host about how it

will permit its communicative property to be used. There is a misconception that this is a First Amendment "freedom of speech" issue—censorship that is equivalent to the government punishing a person for a particular expression. However, under the current constitutional doctrine, it is something more like the equivalent of a publisher deciding not to give someone a column in its newspaper or a private citizen deciding not to let someone put a sign on his lawn that contains a message that is offensive to him. The First Amendment limits only government actors, and a social media company is not the government. Indeed, a social media company enjoys its own First Amendment rights not to have the government require it to associate with speech when it prefers not to do so.

Taking an individual off a platform, removing a group, deleting content— all of these actions are constitutional. Social media companies have broad latitude to create policies on how they will handle speech on their networks. However, this latitude has made politicians and pundits on both the left and right uncomfortable.

Government regulation around media is different in other countries. The United States has robust free speech laws. The Pew Research Center "polled 38 countries around the world in 2015 and found that Americans are more tolerant of free speech than other nationalities. They are also the most supportive of freedom of the press and the right to use the internet without government censorship" (Gray, 2016). Since that poll there has been more discussion on censorship and Internet freedoms in the United States and beyond. Things may shift. Jones said, "The question of government regulation of these platforms is going to be a major issue in the years to come, and thoughtful citizens will want to understand these debates."

How Can Librarians Teach and Advocate for Free Speech Online?

Librarians are advocates of free speech. The American Library Association (ALA) has stated clearly and directly in their policies that libraries must not censor material. The ALA addresses free speech in a document titled "First Amendment and Censorship," found with its Intellectual Freedom resources. They write, "The first amendment's constitutional right of free speech, which is also applied to the states, only prevents government restrictions on speech, not restrictions imposed by private individuals or businesses. Mark Zuckerberg can restrict speech on Facebook because it is a private business and he is not the government" (ALA, 2019).

In the document, they also acknowledge that public schools and libraries have been in legal battles about student access to books and other materials and access to the Internet. But the ALA spells out in the Library

Bill of Rights that "libraries should challenge censorship in the fulfillment of their responsibility to provide information and enlightenment" (ALA, 2020). It can be difficult to challenge censorship. Librarians may be on the receiving end of complaints and criticisms and be pushed to make decisions by bosses, politicians, and parents. But the ALA "First Amendment and Censorship" document reminds librarians that "criticism of the government, political dissatisfaction, and advocacy of unpopular ideas that people may find distasteful or against public policy are almost always safeguarded" (ALA, 2019).

Librarians can teach and advocate for free speech by:

- Promoting campaigns like Banned Books Week to highlight "unpopular ideas" and censorship.

- Model digital etiquette and free speech in their policies. More information about creating these policies is found in the next chapter.

- Reference ALA free speech policies in their internal policies and posters and other materials throughout the library. Another document to share from ALA is its Freedom to Read Statement.

- Teach the First Amendment and digital law. One example to teach this is by celebrating Constitution Day, the day the final draft of the Constitution was signed, September 17, 1787. The Library of Congress has a variety of resources for "Constitution Day" for librarians and educators. (Library of Congress, n.d.)

RonNell Anderson Jones encourages us all to understand how social media's policies affect our speech:

> . . . It would be helpful for people to understand that the private policies that are created by social media companies have a significant impact on their speech. The social media platform that hosts your speech is making content-moderation decisions that determine what the speech environment that you occupy will feel like. These are found in the terms and conditions that you agree to at the time you sign up for an account. It would be helpful if citizens understood the power that is held by major platforms if they thought more carefully about the power that they have as consumers to decide where they engage in speech.

The policies of platforms affect the culture (or, as Jones says, the "environment") and the content. We sign these policies and enter these different "lands" without much former knowledge or understanding. We may find ourselves pulled over on social media for laws we didn't know we broke and laws that we did not have public input on. The ability to understand these laws and cultures is crucial for digital citizens. And the ability to empathize with different messages and audiences is needed more than ever in our polarized world. We are all communicating more than ever, but it's debatable whether we're communicating well. We send messages constantly, but those messages may not be received by our inattentive and distracted audience.

The next chapter will discuss taking our library culture and goals and putting them into policy and practice. Other chapters will discuss practical strategies and lessons for teaching and advocating digital communication. Digital communication is not just important for being a digital citizen, but for being a citizen of the world.

CHAPTER 3

Creating Policies and Best Practices

You probably know what digital citizenship is. Perhaps you already knew before you picked up this book. If not, by this chapter, you should have an understanding of the discipline. But knowledge is just the first step to action. And action on a system-wide scale is difficult. While you may be an expert, your colleagues may know little, or nothing, about digital citizenship. Even if there is a level of knowledge of this concept in your library, what can you do with that knowledge?

When making organizational change, we have to use knowledge to shift norms and values. From those values, we create mission statements, policies, objectives, guidelines, and best practices. This chapter will guide you through some of that process—to embed digital citizenship best practices across a whole branch, from a school to a district, and into a library system. It will offer suggestions to create those guidelines not only with shared values in mind but with an understanding of legal and ethical issues. In this chapter, best practices and policies, both externally and internally, are discussed. If we are not modeling good digital citizenship practices internally, how can we expect our patrons and students to?

Gap Analyses: What Does Your Library Know?

A gap analysis compares two concepts: the reality of where you are with where you want to go. Organizations create gap analyses to determine where they are and forge a path forward. Before working to create large-scale change around digital citizenship, you first must understand where you and your colleagues are around the topic.

A gap analysis helps answer such questions as:

- What are your goals?
- Where are you in relation to your goals?
- What will you do to get there?
- How important is getting there?
- Who is responsible for leading the way?
- Who has ownership of these goals?

Two important parts of the sample gap analysis include "priority" and "ownership." There must be clearly defined priorities when working to create institutional change. If priorities are not indicated—then everything is a priority. The word "ownership" means who is responsible for leading the action. It doesn't necessarily mean that person may be doing the action; they could just be supervising or coordinating it. And it could be a division or a small group instead of an individual. The person responsible tracks and reports progress, follows up on items, and has accountability for the action.

If you create a gap analysis with no ownership, be prepared for no one to volunteer to take it on. While you may have people in your library that are passionate about digital citizenship, for many, it's just one more task on a long list. You can't force people to get excited about institutional change. Many may push back. What's in it for them besides more unpaid work? Why should they be excited just because you are? Jointly making system goals and giving everyone a part divvies out the accountability for reaching those goals. When someone is accountable for action and owns it, they know they have more people depending on them. For example, you're more likely to go to the gym if you have someone waiting for you there. And you're more likely to follow up on your digital citizenship action knowing others are waiting for your report. Progress towards goals can be stalled or even stopped if those two parts, priority and ownership, are not defined.

Once a gap analysis is created, it should be shared systemwide. Goals are not helpful buried in a file or a desk. They must be visible and prominent and a continual reminder of what everyone agreed to.

Organizational Knowledge and Change

Digital citizenship is a multidisciplinary subject that touches many other subjects in a school—or roles in a public library. That is why others outside the library must be a part of creating digital citizenship goals and any gap analyses. Roles in public libraries that can be included in this type of work include:

- Library administrators
- Technology specialists/coordinators
- Youth services librarians
- Marketing and public relations
- Human resources
- Members of outreach teams
- Other leaders in the city/county, library system (i.e., department or division directors, local elected officials), etc.

In schools, digital citizenship touches multiple topics. These intersections will be discussed more in later chapters. But generally, these subjects include some element of digital citizenship:

- Mathematics
- Career and technical education
- English/language arts
- History
- Computer science
- Health science/education

In addition to those subject areas, school librarians should include different staff roles. These involve roles such as principal, assistant principal, school counselors, parent–teacher association (PTA) presidents, school community council members, and parents. More information about communicating and collaborating with the different positions in a school will be discussed in Chapter 6.

As noted numerous times before, librarians have a key role in teaching and advocating digital citizenship. But depending on the organizational structure and culture, they may not be the ones to take a school- or district-wide leadership approach. Every organization needs to examine and decide who takes what ownership. If multiple roles are involved, say a library media specialist and a computer science teacher takes the lead—who makes the final decision? And whom do they report to? A gap analysis can help organizations put all the different roles and subject experts together and decide on ownership so the work moves forward, instead of being siloed in one area.

An example of a systemwide digital citizenship change was Los Angeles Unified School District (LAUSD). In 2015 there were pockets of passion and concerns around the topic of digital citizenship district-wide. But there was no system and district-wide support. Dr. Vanessa Monterosa helped guide the district through this big shift. In doing so she writes, "We learned that you need a strategic change management approach to the following: policies, partnerships, and professional learning" (Monterosa, 2021). When implementing that change in LAUSD, they used the ADKAR Model, which describes certain goals as necessary for change:

- Awareness of the need to change

- Desire to participate and support the change

- Knowledge of how to change

- Ability to implement the change

- Reinforcement to keep the change in place (Monterosa, 2021)

A gap analysis addresses the "knowledge" and "ability" to change. But it cannot create awareness. This awareness often falls to librarians, who may already be teaching digital citizenship in their libraries and have a greater understanding of the topic than their colleagues. Before a gap analysis is even created, there has to be an awareness that creates the desire to change. That desire may take a long time to grow. But librarians can encourage it by sharing articles or anecdotes around digital citizenship, taking time to teach it in classrooms, creating resource lists around it, and having many conversations with colleagues.

Monterosa writes in an article about the digital citizenship shift in LAUSD that some fundamental questions also have to be asked: "Why do we need to change? What is the purpose? Why is this change needed at this time?" (Monterosa, 2021). If someone is not aware of digital citizenship, they won't be able to answer any of those questions. There are numerous answers to those questions, but Monterosa proposes answering them with this response: "The compelling reason guiding the need for an instructional paradigm shift is a district goal for preparing students for a 21st-century workforce. Without a system where leaders model and exemplify 21st-century digital citizenship programs, students will miss out on opportunities to observe and practice real-world skills needed to thrive in an increasingly digital world" (Monterosa, 2021).

Online Privacy

Educating and advocating for online privacy is not only part of digital citizenship but an essential component of a library's mission. The American Library Association (ALA) has always been a privacy activist, both in the halls of Congress and through its other awareness and education campaigns. The ALA's Library Bill of Rights states, "All people, regardless of origin, age, background, or views, possess a right to privacy and confidentiality in their library use" (ALA, 1996). The Bill of Rights also informs online privacy. The ALA has different privacy guidelines for vendors, assistive technology, K–12 schools, and more (ALA, 2019). As technology changes, policies change. For instance, in 2021 the ALA created a "Resolution in Opposition to Facial-Recognition Software in Libraries." That resolution and other statements by the ALA give responsibilities and recommendations to librarians around privacy that include:

- Ongoing privacy education and training to library workers, governing bodies, and users . . .

- Libraries should not monitor, track, or profile an individual's library use beyond operational needs.

- Data collected for analytical use should be limited to anonymous or aggregated data . . .

- Emerging biometric technologies, such as facial recognition, are inconsistent with the mission of facilitating access to library resources free from any unreasonable intrusion or surveillance. (ALA, 2021)

- Libraries should never share users' personally identifiable information with third parties or vendors that provide resources and library services unless the library obtains explicit permission from the user . . .

These are powerful statements and promises to library users. Libraries operate at a higher standard than other businesses or institutions regarding privacy, and these declarations and others make libraries a model to other institutions. But how does this work in practice? And how can we still protect user privacy in the face of more technology than ever before? In an *American Libraries* article in 2019, Marshall Breeding points out this difficulty and contradiction with online privacy:

> In ensuring user privacy, libraries that provide personalized online services often encounter tensions and contradictions. Tools and technologies that offer opportunities for better engagement do not always draw a clear boundary between privacy and personalization. . . . To manage websites and internet technologies in ways that reflect their values, libraries invariably must make difficult choices and compromises. (Breeding, 2019)

School libraries may even face more of these contradictions. With the increase in remote learning and smart tools in the classroom, there are even more third parties competing for student data. In addition, schools in the United States follow the Family Educational Rights and Privacy Act (FERPA). There is debate and different state laws on whether K–12 school library records are considered "education records" and fall under FERPA laws. This means that in some situations parents may be able to access student records on their child's library activity.

As advocates for digital citizenship, libraries must model and pave the way. Creating best practices and policies that respect both the staff and the library's user's privacy is an important step.

Creating Privacy Policies

At a minimum, libraries must have clear, accessible, and prominent privacy policies on their websites. The Federal Trade Commission (FTC) recommends privacy policies for most websites that collect and share consumer data, and some states mandate them. This privacy policy should be regularly updated and included on a footer, header, or separate tab on a website (Free Privacy Policy, 2020). The ALA, for example, has its privacy policy on a footer found on every page (ALA, 2018).

There are numerous places where privacy policies ought to be prominent. Privacy policies should also be on any pages with forms that collect information. Some organizations like news sites have a pop-up message that appears as soon as a user accesses the site with a box that asks you to "Press OK to signify you've read and accepted our Privacy Policy." If the library has an app, the privacy policy should be linked in the app store listing. If there's a separate sign-in page a library uses, like to access a database, the privacy policy must be easily accessed there as well.

What needs to be included in a privacy policy? The Better Business Bureau writes, "You're legally responsible for abiding by the privacy policy promises you make in your policy," so libraries must make sure they write it carefully (Better Business Bureau, 2020). The specific requirements can vary from state to state, so libraries may consider consulting a lawyer before creating one. If a library is part of a larger organization, like a city government or school district, most likely there is a privacy policy previously created they can use. But if a library is creating a website privacy policy from scratch, they should include these issues:

- What data the library collects

- How that data is being collected

- What the library will do with the data

- How customers can control their library data

- How the library protects personal data

- Contact information for the user to access or ask other questions about their data (Better Business Bureau, 2020)

This is just the minimum, and a library may decide to include more details. For example, ALA's privacy policy includes specific provisions for "California Privacy Rights" and how data may be transferred to computers outside the user's state or country (ALA, 2018). In addition to making the policy accessible on the site, it should be written. Write simply without legalese so people of all abilities can understand the policy. For more help check out the ALA's library privacy checklist and other privacy resources at their site Choose Privacy Every Day (chooseprivacyeveryday .org) (Choose Privacy Every Day, 2021).

In addition to online privacy policies for external users, libraries should protect their own staff's privacy. Some questions library policy makers should ask themselves include:

- What tools and platforms are required for internal use?

- Are staff being asked to communicate work matters on private devices?

- Are screenshots of internal communications allowed?

- Can staff forward and share internal emails? If so, are there any that are not allowed?

- Are staff required to have a social media presence as part of their work?

Generally, in the United States, private employers do have the legal right to monitor the email, computers, and phones of their employees. But employers cannot listen in on calls that are placed to and from their locations.

The Electronic Communications Privacy Act (ECPA) prohibits employers from monitoring personal phone calls at a worksite. Employers are also required to let their employees know they may be monitored by cameras on site (Rogers-Whitehead, 2019). These federal laws, like many other laws, have not kept pace with technology. There are legal gray areas around GPS monitoring, what's allowed on employee-owned devices, technologies like biometrics, and tools used to surveil employees that are remote workers (Rogers-Whitehead, 2019). Libraries, as privacy advocates, should make sure they are protecting privacy both internally and externally.

Online Privacy Laws

When crafting online privacy policies in the library, staff should have an understanding of the law. Each state has its variation of online privacy laws. Some state laws may be more comprehensive than others. For example, the California Online Privacy Protection Act (CalOPPA) has additional requirements from websites and apps to protect the privacy of California residents.

In school libraries, there are likely additional privacy laws and regulations. Media specialists not only need to follow federal and state laws but additional rules from their district or state. When adopting new technology in a school library, the vendors for that technology should be following those laws as well. But librarians should do their due diligence to understand the privacy policies of any third-party vendor that provides services to students.

Other privacy laws that may affect libraries include:

- **General Data Protection Regulation (GDPR):** This law was implemented in 2018 and protects the privacy rights of 28 European Union countries. Organizations that control and process data must put in measures to protect it. Individuals must also be content with their data being collected, meaning websites and organizations have to share information about the purpose of their data collection, their retention policy, and if it would be shared outside of Europe.

- **Personal Information Protection and Electronic Documents Act (PIPEDA):** In 2000, Canada adopted this act, governing how private-sector organizations disclose, use, and collect personal information through the course of doing business. PIPEDA is designed to protect Canadian citizens when they're dealing with private businesses, particularly online. It contains special stipulations regarding the language of policies, that the language must be simple enough that children and the mentally impaired can understand it.

Canada also approved the Fighting Internet and Wireless Spam Act in 2010, which requires communications sent by Canadian companies or through Canadian servers to only send emails to those who opt into receiving them.

- **Children's Online Privacy Protection Act (COPPA):** This U.S. federal law, effective as of 2000, imposes requirements and restrictions on data collected for children 13 and under. COPPA does not protect children from potentially predatory advertising or lying about their age to access the content. There are current legislative discussions to amend COPPA to include other types of data that can be collected, such as geolocation information and biometrics.

The FTC regulates online privacy in the United States and the administration of COPPA. So far, they have sued YouTube, Google, and Facebook for violations. In 2019, the FTC, with the New York attorney general, alleged that YouTube channels collected minors' personal information without parental consent. Google LLC and its subsidiary YouTube LLC paid a record $170 million to settle the allegations (FTC, 2019). The FTC also had YouTube change its processes and platform to follow COPPA laws. YouTube announced after the settlement that it would consider data from anyone watching content for children as "coming from a child, regardless of the age of the user" (Wojcicki, 2019). YouTube also stopped providing personalized ads on content and hid some features on kids' channels. Libraries wanting to understand more about privacy laws under the FTC can find it on https://ftc.gov.

Both school and public libraries receive E-rate funding in the United States from the Federal Communications Commission (FCC). The FCC provides discounts for telecommunications and information services in schools and libraries. This can include internal broadband services and the maintenance of those connections. But to qualify for that E-rate funding, libraries "must enforce a policy of Internet safety and certify compliance with the Children's Internet Protection Act (CIPA)" (FCC, 2020). This means that libraries must have some measure of filters for minors and adults. It also means that libraries must have some kind of online safety policy. This requirement is an opportunity to evaluate and expand any digital citizenship policies in the library. Each library gets to decide exactly what content should be blocked. That decision-making process can include conversations on safety and media literacy. These federal requirements for funding may push against online privacy rules. Some public libraries, understandably, may have concerns about the blocking, since the required filters affect adults in addition to minors. But even if a public library does not use filters, it should still evaluate its technology policies.

Other Tips to Protect Student and Patron Privacy

Libraries have long been privacy advocates. Just following the laws should be considered a baseline for online privacy. What other actions can libraries take to protect both student and patron privacy?

- **Ban facial recognition.** In 2021 the American Library Association Council adopted "Resolution in Opposition to Facial-Recognition Software in Libraries." In the resolution, the ALA "opposes the use of facial recognition software in libraries of all types on the grounds that its implementation breaches users' and library worker's privacy and user confidentiality." The resolution called for libraries that may have already adopted this software to "immediately cease doing so based on its demonstrated potential for bias and harm and the lack of research demonstrating any safe and effective use" (ALA, 2021).

- **Use secure browsers.** Not all browsers are created equal. Some, like DuckDuckGo and Brave, do not track the user's history. Other browsers, like Firefox, have many privacy add-ons and plugins that can be used. Google Chrome also offers those add-ons, so libraries may choose to customize a more well-known browser instead of adding the more private ones (Library Freedom Project, n.d.).

- **Require HTTPS.** That "s" on the first part of URLs stands for secure. Sites that use HTTPS have additional layers of security when transferring information. The Electronic Frontier Foundation and the Tor Project developed "HTTPS Everywhere," which is an extension available on most browsers that encrypts communications and makes browsing more secure. This extension is available for free on both desktop and mobile devices (Electronic Frontier Foundation, 2021).

Libraries can, and should, address online privacy through several fronts. They can develop policies that protect their users and staff. Libraries can share those policies on their websites and other locations. They can be diligent in following federal, state, and district laws around privacy. Libraries can also regularly update their technology and add more software to enhance user privacy. And libraries can also protect the user and staff privacy in spaces like social media, which are known privacy violators.

Social Media Policy

During my time as a librarian, I moderated and/or managed nine different social media accounts, including Facebook groups, Instagram accounts, and early in my career, a Myspace page. For most of that time, I had little to no direction or advice. I remember teens advising me on Facebook groups and events, not administration. It wasn't until years after creating and running these accounts that some policies and best practices arose. I had great successes with these accounts, but I also made mistakes. Running those social media groups brought the community to the teens I served, but it also served to dissolve boundaries between my work and personal life. I increased my program attendance but also increased my stress by working extra hours answering DMs (direct messages) at night or having to moderate comments at home. Libraries should craft external and internal social media policies not just to model positive digital citizenship but also to protect their staff and patrons.

Creating External Social Media Policies

Sheena Blauvelt, SHRM-SCP, is an HR director who regularly works with communications policies. She says when libraries are drafting guidelines for staff around social media to ask this important question: What do you want your customer to experience? Libraries need to determine their norms and values around the patron's experience with the library's social media channels. Is your primary motive to share information? Or to create community? Promote programs? All of the above?

Blauvelt advises that all policies be built around the customer experience. She said this

> will help create the acceptable and unacceptable guidelines for their social media practices. Example: Do you want your customer to experience short and automated responses? If yes, something like "Please call 888-123-456" would be acceptable. If no, something like "Hi Jane, we appreciate your feedback. We are doing everything possible to fulfill your request and will reach out to you directly once this item is available" would be more appropriate. Most importantly, know what you are trying to accomplish with your policy.

When creating or updating those social media policies, libraries must determine who takes the lead. This can be a difficult question to answer because there can be many different accounts and library locations. Perhaps another way to look at this question is who is accountable? If there is a social media blunder or a question, who is the person or what is the division that handles it?

There are arguments to be made on the side of centralization and decentralization of social media. In my experience, my local patrons mainly followed their branch accounts. They weren't interested in programs, events, and information from other branches. They wanted to hear from the people they knew and trusted. The teens in my social media groups wanted to interact with the librarians they knew, not a faceless person from the administration. They wanted a level of autonomy and flexibility in their online platforms, to share things in the groups and events, and to joke around. A certain amount of trust is needed for social media community building. Individuals are not interested in talking to generic library accounts, but real people. But on the other side, this decentralization can cause issues such as mixed messaging, more work from (sometimes untrained or inexperienced) staff, lack of cohesive branding, and confusion around accountability and responsibility.

After operating with little to no oversight for years running various large and active groups and accounts, I admit I bristled when new policies and rules were developed. I felt frustrated to have it all come from a small team with no input from staff on the ground. In any organization, there's a push and pull from the top and the bottom. There's a disconnect between the experiences of people working with customers/patrons/students and those who are removed from the public. Libraries should be aware of this gap and be inclusive when developing policies and guidelines. The marketing director should talk to the people involved in the day-to-day running of accounts. There should be a place for open communication and regularly evaluating policies. There also should be some flexibility from the administration. Libraries serve everyone, including people of different ages, ethnicities, abilities, and more. A one-size-fits-all approach to every single social media account is not the best way to focus on the customer experience. Create a certain amount of leeway in your social media policies. A simple sample social media policy template can be found in Appendix C.

Netiquette Guides and Policies

There is confusion between the word "guide" and "policy." Overall, policies are more compulsory than guides. Policies are created from up top. They may originate from a district, state, county, or city. Policies are mandatory, while guidelines are recommended. Policies are often guided by laws or executives, while guidelines are created through best practices. When should a library create a guide instead of a policy? If a library has a clear directive from their bosses of what speech is allowed and what is not, that should be written through a policy. If a library has a *goal* of what speech is allowed and what is not, that's found through a guideline. The issue of netiquette, or digital etiquette, can contain both guidelines and policies. Libraries can encourage positive digital citizenship and clear communication through a guideline. They can discourage hate speech or sexually inappropriate communication through a policy. These policies and guidelines should be created internally and externally. Staff should model positive digital etiquette to students and patrons and abide by similar guidelines.

What should be in a netiquette policy? Sheena Blauvelt recommends that "a netiquette policy should be clear about what is and is not acceptable to share online as well as what is and is not acceptable in terms of communication with customers." She gives some examples of this:

- Do not share any information that is not already available to the public.

- If you are unsure whether or not to share something, check with the manager of public relations (or other contacts).

- Be aware of who your audience is for messaging and data sharing purposes.

A library's privacy policy, which follows state and federal laws, can also be linked to and included in part of a social media policy.

There is more flexibility and subjectiveness when creating guidelines. Guidelines originate from a library's desired goals and norms. While those goals and norms may be influenced or even directed by other agencies, they are also shaped by culture, age, community, language, gender, and class.

For example, the Salt Lake County Library developed a guideline for their Discord server for teens. That guideline stemmed from the main motivation of the group, described by teen librarian Cassie Leclair-Marzolf as "the intention of the program as to be a virtual space for teens to connect, chat, hang out, mess around, and geek out. We wanted it to be a space that was less about having to do something or get something done, and more a place where they could be social together and just be teens" (Rogers-Whitehead, 2021). Like Blauvelt said, before crafting any policy or guidelines, one must ask, "What do I want the customer to experience?" Leclair-Marzolf and her fellow teen librarians wanted the customer, or teens, to experience safety and community. Thus, they included in their Discord guidelines statements such as: "The County Library has a zero bullying tolerance. Bullying is defined as 'unwanted aggressive behavior that involves a real or perceived power imbalance.' (Stopbullying.gov) Social bullying involves leaving someone out." The server also linked to an image saying, "Before you speak, THINK. Is it True? Is it Helpful? Is it Inspiring? Is it Necessary? Is it Kind?" (Rogers-Whitehead, 2021).

Another example of a netiquette guide comes from Anythink Libraries. They clearly lay out in their discussion guidelines their intent and goal: "Anythink is a place that celebrates ideas—in our libraries and our online environments. To keep the Anythink community fun, engaging, and creative, here are some guidelines for joining in our online discussions."

Backing up that goal includes guidelines such as "Share your thoughts—we want to hear from you" and "READ THINK DO—Read the discussions, think about your response, and do publish. But remember, these comments can be read by anyone and will be archived" (Anythink Libraries, 2014). On both of these guideline examples, there's collaborative language— "you, we"—and a desire for participation. When writing guidelines, keep in mind that you're not writing down the law, you're expressing a desire for others to follow a norm your library agrees upon.

Blauvelt said, "Bottom line, all policies should be based on what your organization deems as acceptable and unacceptable." What's acceptable and unacceptable may change. These are norms and values that shift with demographics, management, culture, and technology. Libraries should be open to that change, and by being inclusive with creating guidelines and policies, they can be more aware of those evolving norms.

Creating Internal Social Media Policies

Does your library have any policies regarding staff using social media at work? Do you know them? Are they enforced? Updated regularly? Has your library even considered such a policy? Having some policies around social media can protect both the organization and the users. While I was fortunate in my years running social media accounts at the library to not face harassment or cyberbullying, it could have been different.

There is an increased need for librarians to utilize social media as part of their job. It's a way to communicate with others, promote library pro-grams, find and share information, and more. How can libraries create internal social media policies?

First, Sheena Blauvelt said, a library should determine which staff will use social media. She recommends that it's "better to have assigned staff to interact with the public through social media platforms. From a marketing perspective, this helps the business to have one succinct voice for all in-teractions." From a customer service perspective, however, it may be more efficient to have multiple staff running social media so they can respond quickly to comments and questions. Determining who runs social media depends on what type of library you're part of. A middle-school librar-ian working solo has more need to run an account than a library shelver. A larger library system with a dedicated marketing team may centralize social media more than a small branch. Either way, like Blauvelt, said, having a unified voice is important. Library users should not get multiple answers to the same question.

There are other questions to answer when creating an internal social media policy:

- If staff is required to have a social media profile, what does that profile look like?

- Are staff asked to use their accounts on social media or a generic library account?

- Who or what team determines the social media policy?

- How often are social media policies evaluated?

- How should libraries handle potential online harassment?

- How fast are staff required to answer library users' questions?

- What should librarians do with disagreements, drama, or another incivility on library social media accounts?

In addition to making policy, libraries should offer training on social media. During that training, the policies can be shared and staff can role-play potential scenarios that may occur on accounts. It shouldn't be assumed that librarians are familiar with all social media accounts—not everyone is on Facebook. Running social media accounts should be treated the same as training library staff to use new software or an electronic database. All need a certain level of digital literacy instruction.

Staff training on social media should also include best practices in digital communication. It's not enough to know *how* to communicate; you must also know how to listen. Blauvelt said, "I believe the number one pitfall of digital communication is the inability to hear or visualize tone. One may not know whether a message is being delivered with anger, excitement, sadness, etc." It's easy for both staff and patrons to misinterpret the other.

Evaluating Library Social Media Platforms

What do you want your customer to experience? That's the question to keep in mind when determining policies and guidelines for a library's online channels. But libraries should also consider the platform when looking at the customer experience. As discussed in Chapter 2, every social media platform has a different culture, rules, values, and experiences. Just because your students and patrons are using a platform, that does not mean you need a library account there. Individuals typically use multiple platforms, and there can be more than one communication point between the library and user.

When determining what platforms to use, librarians can ask these questions:

- Is it formal versus informal? What type of language is used on this platform? Is it short, emoji-filled sentences, or longer-form writing?

- Is the platform anonymous or not? The anonymity of some social media, like Reddit, for example, may not make sense for librarians who want to directly communicate with users.

- What age demographic uses this platform? Who is your target market? Parents of preschoolers, teens, seniors, etc., all are likely to use different social media.

Unless a library has specific staff tasked to run social media accounts, trying to reach everyone on most platforms can become a time-consuming task. Libraries who are asking their staff to all participate and run multiple platforms may need to ask themselves: Is this the best use of my staff's time? Perhaps the answer is yes, but continually being logged into social media accounts and having to monitor feeds can cause staff stress.

Libraries should also keep in mind accessibility when utilizing social media platforms. Since libraries provide important information to the public, that information must be accessed by all. The Americans with Disabilities Act (ADA) is the U.S. law that prohibits discrimination based on disabilities. It has three sections, or titles, and Title 2 establishes laws and regulations for public entities like libraries. Those regulations may be physical, like ramps at the library entrance for wheelchairs. But they're also digital. Libraries should make sure their websites are compliant and use third-party sources that follow that compliance. ADA compliance includes rules like having image descriptions and captions, offering plain text on the website that is readable and excludes images, utilizing basic fonts and colors, and having text that dictates and is available for screen readers (User Way, n.d.). If you are unclear whether a social media account is accessible, go look for their accessibility policy or contact them directly. Librarians can also try out the app userway.org to determine if your websites are ADA compliant.

Knowledge is the first step to action. This chapter provided more knowledge on gap analyses, online privacy, and library policy. With that knowledge, library organizations can determine their values around digital citizenship. What is most important for the library? And what kind of experience do libraries want their students and patrons to have? Change in attitudes, values, and behaviors is slow—but technology is not. Libraries and other organizations must be deliberate to keep up with that change.

CHAPTER 4

Programming and Advocacy

Pepper, a 4-foot-tall humanoid robot, is a popular figure with Roanoke County Public Library (RCPL). It greets patrons, answers questions, recommends books, and even dances (Roanoke County VA Government, n.d.). RCPL is the first public library to utilize Pepper, who comes from Japanese SoftBank Robotics in partnership with San Francisco's RobotLab. Library officials say that the goal of utilizing Pepper "is to continue building on the library system's core mission of finding new ways to provide opportunities that are free and available to all" (Petska, 2018). It also promotes and encourages science, technology, engineering, and math (STEM) learning in the Roanoke Valley community.

Pepper is just one of many ways libraries around the world are including digital citizenship in their mission. Curtis Rogers, director of communications with the Urban Library Council (ULC), remarked, "When we talk about digital citizenship at ULC and with libraries it's become such a broad topic that includes all sorts of different things like internet access and emerging tech that it kind of goes all over the place." This broad definition of digital citizenship expands the discussion, but also means it can be difficult for libraries to narrow down what to do around it and how to embed it in their library or school. "As far as the embedding piece," Rogers said, "I'd say it's a new area for libraries." He goes on to add:

> We have libraries that embed emerging tech, VR (virtual reality) for example. There's a program called Magic Leap One, an augmented reality program out

in Miami. There was this great experiment in Cambridge called the Laughing Room . . . basically at the library they had this installation where there was this room with an AI listening to people and sort of laugh track to your conversation. It's such a bizarre interesting, strange way to disrupt what people are thinking. Roanoke County was one of the first libraries in the country to have Pepper, their library staff member. One way to bring the emerging tech conversation in is to have it there. That's a classic strength of libraries in a trustworthy setting to introduce people of all ages to new technology. They had Pepper the robot as a staff member. Pepper is onsite and integrated into programs and around to answer questions and to amuse and entertain and engage kids and teens in conversations about what it means to be.

There is no *one* way to include digital citizenship in libraries. One library may want to emphasize media literacy, others will include coding classes, and others may want a 4-foot-tall dancing robot. This chapter will share programming ideas, aimed at a public library setting, on how to include digital citizenship in library activities and events. More specific library program ideas will be shared in the appendixes and throughout the second half of this book.

This chapter will also delve into topics of digital inclusion and advocacy. Digital citizenship is not a passive term, but an active one. A digital citizen does not just watch the world through their newsfeed but engages in it. And librarians should not just be aware of digital citizenship concepts but work to teach them.

Digital Citizenship Public Library Programming for Children

Children grow up with screens. From their first breath, or even in the womb, their pictures are posted on screens. Screens are in their homes and in their caregivers' hands, and their first exposure is younger than before. An analysis of that exposure published in *JAMA Pediatrics* found a large increase in screen time in the youngest ages, 0 to 2. From 1997 to 2014 screen time grew from 1.32 to 3 hours daily for infants and toddlers. These results, based on diary entries, concluded that for infants, screen time doubled in about 15 years. In the *JAMA* study, most of this screen time was television. The researchers write, "As stakeholders warn against an overreliance on mobile devices they should be mindful that young children spend most of their screen time watching television" (Madigan et al., 2019). There is nothing inherently wrong with screen time, but it's an opportunity cost. If you're watching a screen, you may not be playing with a toy or interacting with a parent. And that cost is high for young developing brains that are learning about the world and language.

Librarians have an opportunity to model screen time use and help parents balance those screens with books and personal interactions. A key part of early literacy is the caregiver/child interaction. The research-based initiative Every Child Ready to Read provides practices and examples for parents to encourage the skills needed to read. These five practices—Read, Write, Talk, Sing, and Play—start at birth (Association for Library Services for Children, n.d.).

Screens can interrupt those early literacy practices. They stand in between "serve and return" interactions. Serve and return interactions are defined by Harvard University's Center on the Developing Child as ones that "shape brain architecture. When an infant or young child babbles, gestures, or cries, and an adult responds appropriate with eye contact, words, or a hug, neural connections are built and strengthened in the child's brain that support the development of communication and social skills" (Harvard University, 2020).

If a parent is singing with a young child and then gets a message on their phone, loses eye contact, stops singing—there's a dead stop to that interaction. If a parent is reading to a child but a television is blaring in the background providing a distraction, that also interrupts the learning. Life happens sometimes, and we have to answer our phones. But if those interruptions happen again and again, the unpredictability of that serve and return response can affect children. The Center of the Developing Brain writes,

> If an adult's responses to a child are unreliable, inappropriate, or simply absent, the developing architecture of the brain may be disrupted, and subsequent physical, mental, and emotional health may be impaired. The persistent absence of serve and return interaction acts as a "double whammy" for healthy development: not only does the brain not receive the positive stimulation it needs, but the body's stress response is activated, flooding the developing brain with potentially harmful stress hormones. (Harvard University, 2020)

Librarians can model these healthy "serve and return" interactions through storytimes for infants, toddlers, and preschoolers. Some ways to do this include:

- Pausing in the story to ask the audience what they think.

- Making eye contact with the children attending storytime.

- Calling out specific children for input or allowing them to participate. A child can hold a prop or put a flannel piece on a board.

- Pointing out words and pictures on the page.

- Giving children noisemakers and leading them in a song.

- Smiling, welcoming, and making eye contact when children arrive.

Parents should be educated on how children's brains develop. Handouts at storytimes can be provided to caregivers illustrating different early literacy practices. A librarian may choose to pause during an activity to tell the parents why they are doing this particular activity and how it relates to literacy. Librarians can give suggestions of books, songs, educational toys, and more for parents to repeat the process at home. More ideas for teaching parents and families will be discussed later in the chapter.

Librarians and caregivers should be aware that screen use continues to shift in children. Since the *JAMA* meta-analyses, Common Sense Media published a survey tracking trends from 2011 to 2020. The surveys followed media use by children under age eight in the United States. There was a switch from television viewing, the largest amount of screen use found in the 2014 study, to online video watching. The Common Sense Media report states, "For the first time, watching online videos on sites like YouTube now constitutes the largest proportion of children's total TV and video viewing, with an average of 39 minutes a day—more than double the amount of time devoted to online videos three years ago (:19)." After online videos, the next most popular form of media in this age group was streaming services. The Common Sense Media surveys found that "more than a third of children age 8 and younger watch online videos every day" (Rideout & Robb, 2020).

There is a wealth of amazing educational videos out there. And librarians should curate and share them. Children's videos and apps are not rated through any kind of vetted and research-based system. Anyone can label a video on YouTube as for children or educational. This is where librarians can step in. Librarians can help parents find the most appropriate videos for their online video–loving children. But they should also keep in mind the amount of screen time young children already have. Parents also may turn to libraries in response to their young children being behind screens. They want alternatives and diversification. They also, although they may not express it, want guidance on what to do.

I know this is what parents say to me. In surveys of over 500 parents my staff and I taught in fall of 2019, they expressed their biggest concerns around children and technology. One of the top three issues was "spending too much time on screens." For younger children, that time expressed on screens potentially has long-term consequences.

The American Academy of Pediatrics (AAP) published a screen time guideline in 2016 with recommendations for young children. The AAP encouraged parents to give children no screens at all if they were under 18 months old. For children two to five years old, the AAP recommends limiting screen use to no more than one hour a day and says, "Find other activities for your children to do that are healthy for their bodies and minds." Infants and toddlers do not learn the same way from screens as preschoolers and older children. They do not make the connection between the screen and real life (Pappas, 2020). Therefore, the AAP recommends parents should "co-view or co-play with your children" (AAP, 2019). Parents can reinforce the learning and activities in screens and make it more relevant and interesting for young, developing brains. Every Child Ready to Read's five practices are intended to be done together. Librarians can give examples of those practices around technology. Here are some examples of positive and healthy screen time with children:

- **Watch videos with them.** Ask what the child thinks of a certain character or plot. Ask your child what they think will happen next.

- **Encourage reading through screen time.** Many children are attracted to books that have their favorite characters. If a child loves to play Minecraft, recommend a Minecraft graphic novel. If Paw Patrol is a preschooler's favorite show, give them a picture book about it.

- **Use screen time to get active.** There are games and shows that get children moving. A library may want to encourage the play of Pokémon Go in the library. This was something my library did. We bought Pokémon lures to bring children into the library and signed them up for summer reading. In addition, there are shows like GoNoodle which have fun dances that could be incorporated into storytime.

Digital citizenship library programs do not require screens, but they can capitalize on them. But beyond screens librarians can educate and advocate for early literacy. They can show healthy practices to caregivers and children. They can provide alternatives to screens and ideas on how to better incorporate screens at home so children can develop digital citizenship skills.

Digital Citizenship Public Library Programming for Teens

A few years ago, I was at a STEM conference aimed at educators in my state. It was our second day there, and I was sitting at a round table of teachers talking about their panels and classes so far. One of the attendees was an eighth-grade science teacher. She had enjoyed the conference and was excited about the strategies to implement STEM in her class. But there was a problem; this teacher had 30-plus middle-schoolers in each of her science classes. She expressed how difficult it was to get a class that size to follow a lecture, let alone conduct a science experiment. She wanted to do more, but she lacked supplies for her class size, and she was concerned if she brought out chemicals and Bunsen burners someone would get hurt. She was by herself with no aides and only one pair of eyes. The science teacher bemoaned the fact that much of her job was behavior control and teaching to the test. While some of the classes she attended at the STEM conference inspired her, she knew that there was little to no way she had the time and ability to actually implement them in the classroom.

This is a situation in which many teachers find themselves. They want to add more tech-related education in their courses and go beyond lectures to active learning. This type of learning can be defined as activity-based, where teachers ask questions and discuss content and there is more back-and-forth engagement between teacher and student. In a 2021 systematic literature review on STEM education in undergraduate courses, the researchers write, "Despite the overwhelming evidence in support of active learning, prior research has found that traditional methods such as lecturing are still the dominant mode of instruction in undergraduate STEM courses. . . . As many as 75% of instructors who have attempted specific types of active learning abandon the practice altogether" (Nguyen et al., 2021). These are *college* instructors working with *adults*. How much harder is it to implement active learning with busy and often-rowdy adolescents?

This is where libraries can come in. They don't need to teach to a test. They can be more flexible with their learning and instruction. With the barriers to this type of active learning in classrooms, many students may be missing out on valuable instruction. Without this education and introduction to STEM, students could also be missing out on future job opportunities. "In the longer term we're seeing huge shifts in the way that STEM job creation is driving a major piece of our economy," said Curtis Rogers. "There are many conversations about the need that our current educational systems are not keeping up. There are absolutely gaps that are causing people, youth, children to have these disproportionate barriers. Children of color, children from low-income areas, children from rural areas, there are many ways the system is not caring for these youth."

Underrepresentation of people of color in STEM fields has long been an issue. A 2021 Pew Research Center analysis still found persistent gaps in the STEM workforce. Only 9 percent of STEM adult workers were black, and 8 percent were Hispanic. Black and Hispanic students also earn STEM degrees less often than other degree recipients (Kennedy et al., 2021). "There needs to be a lot of intentional work across communities," says Rogers. "There is no institution that can own continuous learning. Libraries have always been leaders in informal learning. I predict that there will continue to be a greater, more intentional partnership between education leaders to address the gaps that exist."

Libraries are natural partners in the community. Across the world they stepped up during the COVID-19 pandemic when schools were closed and services were limited. Libraries offered Wi-Fi hot spots or devices, parked their bookmobiles to provide Internet access, and delivered books to students. Libraries are also spaces for adolescents. As public services and community-gathering spaces decline, libraries become that third space for people to gather. Teens in particular need that gathering space. They need a place away from parents and teachers to be with friends, learn, and grow. Libraries can be that space and that place for informal and active learning.

Informal learning is less structured and is learner-driven. It's more relaxed without tests and certifications, and it is not mandatory. This type of learning fits well in a library setting. It's also a place where teens can get involved. Teens can be mentors and models around digital citizenship. Younger children look up to their older peers. They may be more likely to listen to someone a few years older than to an adult. One example of teen teaching with Boston Public Library involves "high-achieving high school students" providing free after-school homework help (Boston Public Library, n.d.). The Cyber Seniors program pairs teens with seniors to teach digital literacy skills. Through that work teens bridge a generational divide and hone their own digital literacy skills by helping others (Rogers-Whitehead, 2016). There are many ways to get teens active and involved in areas of digital citizenship. A sample Minecraft mentor program for teens can be found in Appendix D.

When getting teens involved in mentoring and teaching at the library, consider these tips:

- **Provide ongoing support to mentors.** Librarians should offer training for and regular check-ins on their mentors. Mentors should have a point of contact where they can direct questions and concerns.

- **Prepare for more planning and time.** Having teens teach with library programs means more, not less, time for library programming prep. While the librarian themselves may not be the one running the program, they need to be involved in recruiting teen mentors, advertising the program, setting up and taking down, and more.

- **Give mentors and mentees extra time to get to know each other.** Part of mentorship is not just learning, but the relationship between the mentor and mentee. If a teen is mentoring young people in their library, understand that a certain amount of "getting to know you" and small talk is important. Try to assign the same mentors with the same mentees so they can grow that relationship.

- **Be flexible with schedules.** Teens have after-school activities, jobs, clubs, and other responsibilities. They also may have difficulties with transportation and getting to and from the library. Try to work with their schedule, not yours.

- **Refine recruitment.** Be transparent and open with prospective peer mentors on the responsibilities and time commitment of the work. Consider working with them to create an agreement they will sign. If you have engaged teen mentors already, have them involved in the recruitment process.

The nonprofit the National Mentoring Partnership offers resources and toolkits for organizations wishing to start mentorship programs. In their resources for peer mentorship, they cite some of the benefits of peer mentorship from existing research (MENTOR, n.d.). Some of these benefits include:

- Connectedness to school

- School engagement and retention

- Improvement in grades

- Increased academic achievement

- Improvement with social skills and leadership development

Other findings from peer-reviewed journals suggest that peer mentorship may reduce cyberbullying and social exclusion in middle and high schools (MENTOR, n.d.). When teens volunteer and help at the library, they increase their connection to the place. They have a sense of ownership and belonging, and they want to make that place safer and better for others as well. When people are engaged in their communities, they are also more involved citizens. This real-life attachment and engagement can translate to our online communities. When we feel connected to our organizations and larger community, we can feel more connected to the larger online world. And we can move beyond existing in that digital ecosystem to actively advocating.

Digital Citizenship Public Library Programming for Families

Digital citizenship affects all ages, from infants to seniors. This book emphasizes teaching and advocating digital citizenship to young people. Young people are the audience of school librarians and many public librarians. Library programming also reaches young people in a critical time in their lives, when they're developing social skills and identities, and libraries can reinforce the learning at schools. Despite this book's focus, involving parents and caregivers is important for school and public librar- ies. These are the individuals that will reinforce their child's learning at home and model best practices, and adults need this type of education as well. Concepts such as media literacy, online communication, and digital literacy are ones adults, as well as young people, need to know. Libraries, particularly public ones, have opportunities to expand their audience with digital citizenship programming, potentially making a broader impact.

How can libraries offer digital citizenship programming for families? One idea is hosting a digital parenting program. Parents are hungry for advice, community, and resources around technology in the home. Libraries can bring in partners or individuals to teach adults. For example, a library could bring in a financial expert to talk about online scams. Or even have a teen teach adults about how to use different social media platforms. Libraries could just simply have an open discussion around technology. These discussions can focus on different elements of digital citizenship or encourage digital literacy. When COVID-19 hit and millions of students were sent home with laptops, some parents were left wondering what to do. A family tech night can help train parents on different software and hardware that their children may be using. This may also be a natural partnership between a public library and their local school. For more specifics on hosting a digital parenting event at your library, see a sample digital parenting event in Appendix E.

The area of digital literacy is one in particular where libraries are set up and ideal to teach. Shauna Edson is the digital inclusion coordinator at the Salt Lake City Public Library (SLCPL). Her library system has of- fered digital literacy support and classes since the mid-2000s. She says that there are many ways libraries can encourage digital literacy. "Libraries have public computer labs, computer classes, Creative Labs, and Maker Spaces, and many libraries circulate devices and/or hot spots." During the COVID-19 pandemic Edson and the staff at SCLPL faced difficulties with their work in digital inclusion. "One of the biggest challenges unique to this pandemic is that public computer labs have closed to the public and community members do not have a place to access public computers and in-person one-on-one computer help. . . . It is much easier to work with people in person than over the phone or video conferencing." Most library programming is more difficult online, but particularly digital literacy pro- grams. It can be hard to explain concepts and tasks when you can't see the person or the device. And it was even more difficult for many parents try- ing to figure out how to navigate online homework and laptops with little to no in-person instruction.

A grant from the Institute of Museum and Library Services helped Edson and SLCPL address the challenge of the lack of face-to-face instruction in 2020. This Digital Navigator program was done over the phone or in-person with social distancing. "The City Library recognizes the life changing significance of access to digital resources, and Digital Navigators can help connect patrons to free or low-cost internet services and devices, and help with basic computer skills and training, including navigating the internet, online privacy and security, and more." Edson says they learned a lot from the program and how important the service was to the people they served. One participant said, "I'm pretty excited, this is opening up the world for me. You'll never know how much I appreciate this. I need to stay in touch with what's going on in the world." Another said, "First computer ever! I have a lot to learn. Thank you for helping me during this time of pandemic. I have been overwhelmed that everything is digital."

Even when a pandemic is not raging and keeping people in their homes, "digital" is here to stay. Libraries continue to have an important role in connecting, teaching, and providing access to their communities.

Digital Inclusion and the Digital Divide

Libraries have always been places to educate and advocate for digital literacy. Shauna Edson defines digital literacy as the "skills and knowledge needed to learn, work, play, communicate, participate in our digital society, and assess digital media critically." She also adds the importance of soft skills in digital literacy such as "a sense of belonging and familiarity with technology." Digital literacy is part of the concept of digital inclusion. The National Digital Inclusion Alliance (NDIA) describes digital inclusion as "the activities necessary to ensure that all individuals and communities, including the most disadvantaged, have access to and use of information and communication technologies" (NDIA, 2020).

The NDIA lists five elements of digital inclusion:

- Affordable broadband Internet service
- Devices that can access the Internet
- Access to digital literacy training
- Technical support
- Applications and online content designed to enable and encourage self-sufficiency, participation, and collaboration (NDIA, 2020)

Digital inclusion is necessary for digital citizenship. One element of digital citizenship is access, and access is equitable for everyone. Pew Research found that 17 percent of Americans only have access to the Internet through a smartphone. For low-income households, that percentage is 26 percent (Pew Research Center, 2020). Broadband speeds vary on region and income. The Federal Communications Commission (FCC) estimates over "18 million people lack access to broadband, including 20.7% in rural areas." Other estimates out of the FCC with BroadbandNow Research thinks that 42 million Americans "do not have the ability to purchase broadband internet." In the BroadbandNow report they said that technologies such as fiber and cable are overreported, and many people who did have broadband did not have the higher speeds needed to fully participate online (Busby et al., 2021).

This gap between those that have access, digital literacy skills, and devices is termed the digital divide. Edson says libraries are important to bridge this divide. "Libraries are long-standing anchor institutions for digital literacy and digital inclusion. They are often one of the only places individuals can go to access a free computer lab, charging stations, public Wi-Fi and a cozy spot to settle in with a laptop for the afternoon."

There are far-researching consequences for people who are not digitally included. These became even more evident during the COVID-19 pandemic lockdown, which led Edson and SLCPL to start the Digital Navigators program. Use of data on wireline networks was 47 percent greater in March 2020 than in March 2019 (Busby et al., 2021). With more companies moving to remote work permanently, the need for robust broadband networks and more access will most likely continue. When people don't have networks, devices, or digital literacy skills, they can be shut out of the economy and life. Shauna Edson said:

> Individuals that do not have access to technology or support in using technologies can find it difficult to apply for jobs, access educational opportunities, chat and video conferences with friends and family, share photos and videos, and access health records and telehealth. Small businesses use social media to promote and gain support from their communities. Students are able to learn remotely and participate in group activities through video chat. People that grow-up with computers and technologies in their homes are more familiar with technology and are more likely to use technology in new and innovative ways. Many people have stories about their first computer or interaction with technology as a child, but there are also lots of people who are using technology for the first time as an adult. As technology and adoption continue to advance, so do the digital divides.

How can libraries create programming around digital literacy to help bridge the digital divide? Edson suggested librarians start with "collecting impact stories. Have public service staff members start tracking the time they spend helping patrons on computers, answering questions about technology and/or devices, and program attendance." Libraries can also gather data from their city, county, district, or census and FCC data. State- and city-level data can also be found on the National Digital Inclusion Alliance's site.

After examining what's happening outside the library in terms of digital literacy and inclusion, look internally. Edson recommends, "What is already being done and how can your program support the talent, skills, and interests of your community members?" In some communities the needs are greater than others. Does your library have the staff to support those needs? Is that staff trained on teaching digital literacy and using technology? Does your library have enough devices and fast enough network speed to support those needs?

Next, present a plan to management. This plan can include that gap analysis, seeing what the library has in terms of staff, devices, and resources. When looking at getting buy-in from management, consider a pilot project. "Pilot projects are rooted in experimentation and learning," Edson said, "and are much easier to gain buy-in than a larger project that is new to your organization. If the pilot demonstrates a positive impact it is much more likely to receive the necessary funding to launch a long-term sustainable program."

In addition, consider partners. These partners can be school districts, nonprofits, government officials, and even the private sector. Comcast, AT&T, and other private businesses may be able to sponsor or grant funding. Private and public partners can work together on digital inclusion. For example, in Provo, Utah, the Utah County Digital Inclusion Committee is composed of people from the city, three local school districts, the United Way, Google Fiber, and a local IT company. They work to organize IT volunteers, distribute computers, and advocate for digital inclusion (Pugmire, 2020). Libraries are natural partners for this type of collaborative work. Other organizations have recognized this, including the Nonprofit Technology Network (NTEN), which has housed digital inclusion fellows in libraries around the United States (NTEN, 2021). Edson previously was a NTEN digital inclusion fellow with SLCPL, and that work led the library system to determine they needed a full-time digital inclusion specialist.

Access and inclusion are the baseline for digital citizenship. It is where digital citizenship starts and where it can end. Libraries continue to play a crucial role in providing that access and education to help future digital citizens.

Advocating Digital Citizenship

Diana Veiga is the civic engagement coordinator with District of Columbia (DC) Public Libraries. She was hired into that position after the DC council passed a law that made libraries into official voter registration agencies. This was a new role for libraries, and Veiga was tasked with creating that process. But she ended up doing so much more. Veiga described her role after voter registration:

> That was my first main task, and at the time the Census was happening in 2020, so I sat on Mayor Bowser's complete county committee through 2019 and 2020 and we had grandiose plans for libraries to be centers for people to come in and complete their census since it was going to be online for the first time. So, I worked with staff at branches for them to develop a plan. . . . But then COVID hit and the pandemic happened so we had to readjust.

> Then it was the election, obviously, for 2020 so my other major project just to provide information. We worked closely with the board of elections and they did virtual programs before the primaries and the general elections informing people what would happen. By the time we got to the general election they had decided to have mail in ballot boxes in the city. They had them outside every library location. So, the library served as a place people could drop off their ballots. That was a major change. We had to get staff and the city prepared. I created election 2020 page for our website that provided people general information about where they could get their ballots.

> Then for the 2020 election I did two programs, one on voter suppression: we screened the documentary *Suppress: The Right to Vote*. Then I partnered with Storydistrict which is a local storytelling organization and we did a storytelling called "I Too Sing America." because it was 100 years since women got the right to vote and 50 years since the Voting Rights Act.

Veiga has a unique role in libraries, one that continues to evolve. After the 2020 elections she put on a monthly series called "Our City, Our Stories" to focus on local government and governance. She's had presentations by DC Vote since Washington, DC is exploring statehood and helped teach teens how bills become laws. In summer 2021 the DC public library, still mostly virtual, is hosting tenants' rights workshops and youth workshops on writing called "Know Your Power." Veiga is also leading "Civic Engagement 101 Summer Session" programs online, bringing in community activists, authors, and more (DCPL, 2021). "I think it's important that these issues are ongoing and it's not just something we should care about during election," Veiga said. "I want to help people become advocates for themselves and their community."

Veiga's job title and responsibilities are unique in public libraries, but the role of libraries as places for civic engagement are not. As former American Library Association (ALA) president Nancy Kranich describes in her article on "Libraries and Civic Engagement," Ben Franklin founded the first public library, and he saw them as a place for the average citizen, not the aristocracy or religious institutions. Kranich concludes in her article:

> Repositioning libraries as informal civic learning agents fits the theory and practice of community inquiry conceived a century ago by John Dewey (1916). Dewey believed that people need the opportunity to share ideas through multiple media in order to understand and solve everyday problems together. . . . Whether face-to-face or virtual, libraries build learning communities that bring people with mutual interests together to exchange information and learn about and solve problems of public concern. (Kranich, 2012)

The Internet allows us all to connect together more and solve problems. That's what digital citizens do; they don't just passively look at information, they engage in it. Digital citizens are not just consumers of information, they're producers. They're also advocates who speak up.

Civic Engagement Library Programs

How do libraries get more civically engaged? Where do they start? What types of programs should they run? Veiga recommended figuring "out what matters in their community." She gives an example from DC Public Libraries. "DC is not a state . . . politics are local. . . . All we have is local politics." Thus, Veiga and the DC Public Library's focus has been more on local issues, like DC statehood.

Veiga also suggests asking two questions: "What kind of change would people like to see?" and "What organizations are already doing the work?" Libraries are ideal platforms for other advocates, nonprofits, activists, and more. "I don't think you have to reinvent the wheel but bring in people who are doing the work and give them a platform and space to share," Veiga said. For example, Chicago Public Library has hosted "On the Table" citywide events hosted by librarians and at libraries. Tens of thousands of people have participated, talking across the table and listening to others about local challenges and issues (CPL, 2018).

Another way to start with civic engagement is through collections and book displays. "All through the election we had a reading list of children, youth and adult books to complement the website, to complement the programs," said Veiga. These book displays can be on social issues, celebrating different heritages like Black History Month or Asian American and Pacific Islander Heritage Month. Veiga said, "When you do a book display, you're selecting information people should know. And you don't know who's going to pick up that book and who's world might be changed and how you might spark somebody's interest."

Digital citizenship and civic engagement go together. In the 2018 article, "Public Libraries as Platforms for Civic Engagement," the authors write: "Our civic institutions will be stronger if community members can recognize 'fake news,' navigate and participate online, and take action to protect against technological threats. With the right civic engagement efforts, public libraries might become the recognized leaders in distinguishing fact from fake and promoting digital literacy." In the article, along with encouraging digital literacy programs, the writers recommend that "libraries can take a lead role in fighting major threats to civic engagement and to society in general by designing programming that helps navigate the threats posted by modern technology" (Coward et al., 2018). Some threats listed include:

- Artificial intelligence and automation

- The Internet of Things (IoT) as security threats

- Data mining and manipulation

The authors did note another challenge to civic engagement, lack of training for librarians (Coward et al., 2018). Therefore, before beginning a civic engagement program, libraries should evaluate their own strengths and weaknesses of staff. This type of training is not part of library science programs and media specialist certifications. Libraries should also look at their own resources and time and determine if they have enough staff to meet demand.

Youth services librarians and school media specialists play an important part in civic engagement for young people. It's work more of them have done in recent years. In a 2020 *American Libraries* article, "Let Them Lead," efforts of teen librarians around the United States in civic engagement were described (Udell, 2020). At Waltham Public Library (WPL) in Massachusetts, a program, Real Talk, was founded by a local teen in 2016. The goal of the group was to "help youth develop their own voices within a social and emotional learning environment where they can explore issues affecting their community" (Waltham Public Library, n.d.). The groups are teen-led, and teens have used that platform to reach out to the mayor, local representatives, and the larger public. The teens, with staff at WPL, also developed modules and activity guides for libraries to start similar programs at https://sites.google.com/minlib.net/real-talk-teens/home.

This type of advocacy work builds skills in teens. One important skill for digital citizenship is self-efficacy, one's belief in their own abilities and capabilities to control themselves. For someone to create, to advocate, they need to have that confidence in their own work, which can inspire them to share and speak out. Civic engagement programs in libraries help build self-efficacy. Virginia Walter, the author of *Young Activities and the Public Library*, said about library programming around social issues: "The kids have firsthand experience with a lot of these issues. One of the key ingredients in this is a sense of efficacy. That's something that a library can be involved with" (Udell, 2020).

Diana Veiga has created and hosted civic engagement programs like this for young people. She and others of the DC Public library staff recruited poll workers for the 2020 election. She said, "We need to get their voices heard. They want to be involved and active in the community." Veiga would like to start freedom schools for children in the library with the Children's Defense Fund program. She said, "I think it's important that systemwide library systems are making the decision to encourage civic engagement participation from kids on up."

Public libraries are liked and well-known community institutions with space, staff, and resources. As Nancy Kranich writes, "Libraries have long recognized their role in promoting access to a diversity of ideas, serving as depositories for government, community, and other useful information" (Kranich, 2012). But more than a repository, there is trust by the public. "I think the library is one of the few places that most people still trust," said Veiga. "I think we have a responsibility."

There are many ways to include digital citizenship in libraries. One branch may decide to focus on digital literacy, another library may want a teen-led social issue discussion group. There's not a right or wrong way. But libraries should keep in mind the issues of access and advocacy. The first step to creating a digital citizen is getting that person online. And digital citizens do not just consume, they create and advocate and are active participants in their real-life and online worlds. More suggestions and activities on including digital citizenship in libraries, with an emphasis on school libraries, will be shared throughout the rest of this book. Additional ideas and lessons can be found in the appendixes.

Librarians are not just curators of information, but creators as well. You have a role in advocating and teaching digital citizenship, not just learning about it. Libraries are third spaces, modern-day town squares, and a trusted resource for many. Libraries lead on topics of literacy and information; they can also move to the forefront of digital citizenship.

CHAPTER 5

Implementing Digital Citizenship in Public Schools

Digital citizenship has been an integral part of our educational practice in one form or another for almost two decades. What started as device management and basic functionality lessons quickly evolved into full-on integration in every aspect of school life. Everyone needs digital citizenship skills. Students, teachers, paraprofessionals, nurses, and building and district administrators all needed to quickly learn how to migrate all aspects of education online. And that was before a global pandemic left us with only virtual solutions to very pressing problems.

The first memory I (Amy) have of my sixth-grade students using devices was a weekly 45-minute trip to the computer lab. I would run around the room trying to help students log in, use a mouse, find where letters were on a keyboard, and open a browser. There is not a starker contrast to the beginning of my teaching career than the arrival of March 2020. The pandemic and distance learning opened a whole new era of education where teaching and learning for us were 100 percent online. From computer labs to 1:1 devices, digital citizenship has always been a part of my 17 years in public education. It has enhanced my teaching career and my students' achievements. I went from telling students how to find letters on a keyboard to teaching students why screencasting on a screen while a teacher is teaching is not advisable.

In some ways, students are more tech-savvy than the teachers and librarians around them, but in more ways than not, they lack the skills to be quality digital citizens and critical problem solvers in their technical lives.

My (Lindi) teaching journey started in 2010, and throughout those 12 years, I held three distinct roles in my district: a high school English teacher, an instructional technology coach, and now a high school librarian. Working at both the district and campus levels, I have been privy to the technology integration process across our entire district, and the higher the integration went, the better we understood the digital citizenship needs of our students and ourselves. Social media became an instructional tool instead of a classroom management issue, computer labs were replaced with flexible learning spaces and mobile devices, tracking student learning data became a daily task, and stacks of paperwork quickly turned into the bottomless pit that is cloud storage. (Side note: Let's all take a mindfulness moment and accept that we will never organize our cloud storage and fully embrace the "search all files" feature. We are still valuable even if we can't remember which sub-sub-folder has that slide deck we need!) Being on the front lines as digital learning has quickly morphed into business as usual because of the COVID pandemic has further convinced me that educators cannot teach what we do not know. When we try, we apply old solutions to new situations. That is why I think the prevailing answer to smartphones and social media in the early 2000s was to outlaw them in acceptable use policies (AUPs). Even for school staff. We didn't know how to teach students to manage their digital lives because we didn't have digital lives of our own. We must change.

The goal with these chapters is to help both school and public librarians guide students and staff to become educated digital citizens. People, no matter their age, must be empowered to manage their own digital lives and not have others fixing problems for them when they arise.

There are many books and websites about why digital citizenship is important. There are not very many that provide ideas about how to implement it. We hope that the plans and processes in these chapters will help you build and keep a digital citizenship program in your school and community thriving and relevant.

SCHOOL LIBRARIES: ESTABLISHING A CURRICULUM

The following sections are designed as a roadmap detailing how to take the concepts and skills from this book and create a digital citizenship program/curriculum that is both comprehensive and multifaceted. For those brand new to digital citizenship, this map will provide as detailed planation as possible about *how* to integrate digital citizenship i library. For those already on the digital citizenship journey, the hope is that this section is a repository of resources and ideas that can inspire new approaches to the burgeoning field of digital citizenship practice.

Digital Citizenship Curriculum

Just like any other skill set, digital citizenship is most effective when it is presented contextually and scaffolded from fundamentals to complex concepts. Just like in math, where students need to learn to add, subtract, multiply, and divide before tackling quadratic equations, students need to learn digital etiquette and safety before jumping into digital law. While it is tempting to go straight to a lesson on copyright or cyberbullying in reaction to an event in the community or on the news, often this approach lacks the context and structure to make lasting behavioral change. Instead, start by finding or creating a digital citizenship scope and sequence to help guide library programming and co-teaching.

Since the field of digital citizenship is early in its development, many key players in both education and technology are putting out content to support students, educators, and parents in mastering the skills of digital life. Companies like Google, Facebook, and Common Sense Media, as well as educational associations such as the American Library Association (ALA) and the International Society of Educational Technology (ISTE), are all investing time, money, and research into creating programs with lesson plans, videos, and activities. These prepackaged programs are a great place to start developing a digital citizenship practice, especially for library programming.

Premade Curricula

Given the multifaceted roles of both school and public librarians, starting with a premade digital citizenship curriculum is often the easiest and best place to start a digital citizenship journey. These programs often include a scope and sequence that make it easy to integrate into existing library programming. It also makes it easier to add on more in-depth lessons on specific elements based on the needs of students or communities. Premade programs are also helpful because they are self-contained and do not require the context of other subject areas such as English or social studies. Instead, librarians can be the driving force of the program without having to rely on outside support. Here are four examples of reputable curriculums that are easy to implement through library programming:

- Berkman Klein Institute—https://cyber.harvard.edu/
- Common Sense Media—https://www.commonsensemedia.org/

- Google's Be Internet Awesome—https://beinternetawesome.withgoogle.com/
- Digital Respons-Ability—https://respons-ability.net/

All of these quality curriculums are thorough, detailed, and well crafted. They make it easy for the public and school librarians to integrate lessons and establish a digital citizenship culture with students, parents, and the community. As the digital citizenship education community continues to grow and evolve, programs such as these will come and go or innovate to keep up with new theories or best practices. It is important to stay informed and adjust the curriculum as needed.

DIY Curriculums

Another approach to digital citizenship integration is to craft an individualized curriculum, rather than implementing an existing one. While this creates more work up-front, developing a tailored digital citizenship curriculum allows for more scaffolding, context, and differentiation for the specific community it serves. This is especially true in school and academic libraries, where embedding digital citizenship skills into collaborative lessons with other academic subjects is often an expectation.

ISTE Standards

ISTE standards are international, created by educators, and applicable to all age levels. They incorporate essential knowledge and skills for good digital citizenship. If your state has digital citizenship standards, use those in addition to or instead of ISTE.

Digital Citizenship: Students recognize the rights, responsibilities, and opportunities of living, learning, and working in an interconnected digital world, and they act and model in ways that are safe, legal, and ethical.

- *2A—Students cultivate and manage their digital identity and reputation and are aware of the permanence of their actions in the digital world.*

- *2B—Students engage in positive, safe, legal, and ethical behavior when using technology, including social interactions online or when using networked devices.*

- *2C—Students demonstrate an understanding of and respect for the rights and obligations of using and sharing intellectual property.*

- *2D—Students manage their personal data to maintain digital privacy and security and are aware of data-collection technology used to track their navigation online.*

(ISTE, 2021)

Example: "Digital Citizenship Scope and Sequence"

Here is an example of an aligned scope and sequence developed for this book. It is based on current standards and research and spans grades K–12. While this is not an exhaustive list of digital citizenship concepts and skills, it is meant to serve as a guide for a more extensive and exhaustive curriculum for K–12 school libraries or other libraries serving youth and their caregivers.

Digital Citizenship Scope and Sequence K–5

Month	Element	ISTE Standard	Key Words/ Key Concepts
August	*Digital Security*	2d Students manage their personal data to maintain digital privacy and security and are aware of data-collection technology used to track their navigation online. (ISTE, 2021)	• Password • Two-factor authorization • Sign on/sign off • Sharing/privacy • Safety • Permission – borrowing from parents/siblings
September	*Digital Literacy*	2c Students demonstrate an understanding of and respect for the rights and obligations of using and sharing intellectual property. (ISTE, 2021)	• Acceptable use policy (AUP) • Device/technology basics
October	*Digital Etiquette*	2b Students engage in positive, safe, legal, and ethical behavior when using technology, including social interactions online or when using networked devices. (ISTE, 2021)	• Manners, how do we treat people in real life (IRL) vs. online • Appropriate vs. inappropriate • Positivity • Cyberbullying • See something, say something
November	*Digital Communication*	2a Students cultivate and manage their digital identity and reputation and are aware of the permanence of their actions in the digital world. (ISTE, 2021)	• Digital footprint • Permanence • Search history • Portrayal/what does it mean to have an identity – which things represent that online?

(Continued)

Digital Citizenship Scope and Sequence K–5 (*Continued*)

Month	Element	ISTE Standard	Key Words/ Key Concepts
December	*Digital Health & Wellness*	2b Students engage in positive, safe, legal, and ethical behavior when using technology, including social interactions online or when using networked devices. (ISTE, 2021)	• Screen time • Workspace • Permission • Mindfulness
January	*Digital Commerce*	2b - Students engage in positive, safe, legal, and ethical behavior when using technology, including social interactions online or when using networked devices. (ISTE, 2021)	• Media literacy • Analyzing an ad • YouTube ads – appropriate or free? • In-game advertisement/ purchasing
February	*Digital Access*	2c Students demonstrate an understanding of and respect for the rights and obligations of using and sharing intellectual property. (ISTE, 2021)	• Global • Community • Empathy • Shared space • Money – what do students have, what do they not have financially?
March	*Digital Rights & Responsibilities*	2c Students demonstrate an understanding of and respect for the rights and obligations of using and sharing intellectual property. (ISTE, 2021)	• Rights • Privileges • Sharing • Fact-checking • Intellectual property/ ownership • Responsibility • Fairness • Copyright • Shared space • Obligation (fourth to fifth) • Understood rules • Community guidelines • Censorship

(Continued)

Digital Citizenship Scope and Sequence K–5 (*Continued*)

Month	Element	ISTE Standard	Key Words/ Key Concepts
April	*Digital Law*	2c Students demonstrate an understanding of and respect for the rights and obligations of using and sharing intellectual property. (ISTE, 2021)	• Ownership • Copyright • Shared space
May	*Digital Law/ Digital Rights & Responsibilities/ Health & Wellness/ Etiquette*		• Screen time • Fact-checking • Just right • Ownership • Ethics

Digital Citizenship Scope and Sequence 6–8

Month	Element	ISTE Standard	Key Words/ Key Concepts
August	*Digital Security*	2d Students manage their personal data to maintain digital privacy and security and are aware of data-collection technology used to track their navigation online. (ISTE, 2021)	• Sharing/privacy • Safety • Personal data • Data collection • Digital footprint • Search history • Algorithm • Filter bubble
September	*Digital Literacy*	2c Students demonstrate an understanding of and respect for the rights and obligations of using and sharing intellectual property. (ISTE, 2021)	• Acceptable use policy (AUP) • Intellectual property • Sharing – how to respect the rights of others while you're sharing • Digital creation • Digital commons • Royalty-free

(*Continued*)

Digital Citizenship Scope and Sequence 6–8 (*Continued*)

Month	Element	ISTE Standard	Key Words/Key Concepts
October	*Digital Etiquette*	2b Students engage in positive, safe, legal, and ethical behavior when using technology, including social interactions online or when using networked devices. (ISTE, 2021)	• In real life vs. Online • Upstander – positivity for all • Complicit • Fact-checking • See something, say something • Cyberbullying • Etiquette during dissent
November	*Digital Commerce*	2d - Students manage their personal data to maintain digital privacy and security and are aware of data-collection technology used to track their navigation online. (ISTE, 2021)	• Media literacy • Analyzing an ad – validity of claims of products – who is running the ad? • Where to find good product reviews/Yelp reviews • Fact-check it • In-game advertisement/ purchasing – gambling – addiction • Algorithms – people use your digital footprint to sell you stuff • Cookies
December	*Digital Communication*	2b Students engage in positive, safe, legal, and ethical behavior when using technology, including social interactions online or when using networked devices. (ISTE, 2021)	• Fact-checking • Digital footprint • Permanence • Search history • Who are you online/ authentic self
January	*Digital Health & Wellness*	2A - Students cultivate and manage their digital identity and reputation and are aware of the permanence of their actions in the digital world. (ISTE, 2021)	• Self-regulate • Ergonomics • Mindfulness • Self-assessment • Blue light • Dopamine reinforcement • Habits

(*Continued*)

Digital Citizenship Scope and Sequence 6–8 (*Continued*)

Month	Element	ISTE Standard	Key Words/ Key Concepts
February	*Digital Rights & Responsibilities*	2c Students demonstrate an understanding of and respect for the rights and obligations of using and sharing intellectual property. (ISTE, 2021)	• Rights and privileges • Sharing (social media) • Fact-checking • Intellectual property/ownership/copyright • Responsibility/obligation • Fairness • Shared space • Understood rules/community guidelines • Censorship
March	*Digital Law*	2c Students demonstrate an understanding of and respect for the rights and obligations of using and sharing intellectual property. (ISTE, 2021)	• Intellectual property • Ownership • Copyright • Rules
April	*Digital Access*	2c Students demonstrate an understanding of and respect for the rights and obligations of using and sharing intellectual property. (ISTE, 2021)	• Global • Community • Empathy • Shared space • Access • Money • Internet as a right
May	*Digital Law/ Digital Rights & Responsibilities /Health & Wellness/ Etiquette*		• Screen time • Fact-checking • Just right • Ownership • Ethics

Digital Citizenship Scope and Sequence 9–12

Month	Element	ISTE Standard	Key Words/ Key Concepts
August	*Digital Security* *Digital Literacy*	2d Students manage their personal data to maintain digital privacy and security and are aware of data-collection technology used to track their navigation online. (ISTE, 2021) 2b Students engage in positive, safe, legal, and ethical behavior when using technology, including social interactions online or when using networked devices. (ISTE, 2021)	• Data management/ identity theft • Algorithm • Password management/ encryption • Freedom of speech vs. freedom of consequences
September	*Digital Communication* *Digital Etiquette*	2c Students demonstrate an understanding of and respect for the rights and obligations of using and sharing intellectual property. (ISTE, 2021) 2b Students engage in positive, safe, legal, and ethical behavior when using technology, including social interactions online or when using networked devices. (ISTE, 2021)	• Disinformation • Fake news • Etiquette during dissent • Trolling • Comment sections • Cancel culture • Advocacy
October	*Digital Law*	2b Students engage in positive, safe, legal, and ethical behavior when using technology, including social interactions online or when using networked devices. (ISTE, 2021)	• Intellectual property/ ownership/copyright • Social media marketing • Terms of service • Community guidelines

(Continued)

Digital Citizenship Scope and Sequence 9–12 (*Continued*)

Month	Element	ISTE Standard	Key Words/ Key Concepts
November	*Digital Commerce*	2a Students cultivate and manage their digital identity and reputation and are aware of the permanence of their actions in the digital world. (ISTE, 2021)	• Read and write product reviews/Yelp reviews • Fact-check it • Expert vs. influencer • Digital banking • Micro-loans (buy now, pay later) • Cryptocurrency • NFT (nonfungible tokens) • Digital investing
December	*Digital Commerce*	2b Students engage in positive, safe, legal, and ethical behavior when using technology, including social interactions online or when using networked devices. (ISTE, 2021)	• Algorithms • Selling personal information • Buying personal information
January	*Digital Health & Wellness*	2d Students manage their personal data to maintain digital privacy and security and are aware of data-collection technology used to track their navigation online. (ISTE, 2021)	• Health tracking • Health data • Planning apps • Telemedicine • Time management • Self-regulation • Addiction/dopamine • Mindfulness
February	*Digital Rights & Responsibilities*	2c Students demonstrate an understanding of and respect for the rights and obligations of using and sharing intellectual property. (ISTE, 2021)	• Rights and privileges • Fact-checking • Responsibility/ obligation • Fairness • Shared space • Censorship • Consequences of copying intellectual property • Transparency

(*Continued*)

Month	Element	ISTE Standard	Key Words/ Key Concepts
March	*Digital Communication*	2c Students demonstrate an understanding of and respect for the rights and obligations of using and sharing intellectual property. (ISTE, 2021)	• Professional social media • Online image • Professional portfolios • Digital branding • Digital identity • Professional communication • Email • SLACK
April	*Digital Access*	2c Students demonstrate an understanding of and respect for the rights and obligations of using and sharing intellectual property. (ISTE, 2021)	• Algorithms • Internet as a right • Marginalized voices online • Activism • Advocating for others and self • Information access
May	*Digital Law* *Digital Rights & Responsibilities* *Health & Wellness* *Etiquette*		• Screen time • Fact-checking • Just right • Ownership • Ethics

Standards Analysis

Following are the elements from Mike Ribble's *Digital Citizenship in Schools*. Originally published in 2007, these nine elements often serve as the foundation for other evolving standards and practices. See the introduction to this book for more information about standards, definitions, and concepts of digital citizenship.

Nine Elements of Digital Citizenship

1. Digital Access
2. Digital Commerce

3. Digital Communication

4. Digital Literacy

5. Digital Etiquette

6. Digital Law

7. Digital Rights and Responsibilities

8. Digital Health and Wellness

9. Digital Security (Ribble, 2015)

The nine elements can be found throughout this book as different digital citizenship concepts are discussed. For example:

Digital Citizenship: Media Literacy and Digital Law

- Digital Literacy

- Digital Law

- Digital Rights and Responsibilities

- Digital Security

- Digital Commerce

Digital Citizenship: Communication and Etiquette

- Digital Communication

- Digital Etiquette

Digital Citizenship: Digital Modeling and Policies

- Digital Health and Wellness

- Digital Access (Ribble, 2015)

In their Standards for Students, ISTE has four digital citizenship sub-standards that have evolved to lead students in transformative learning with technology.

When analyzing a standard, it's important to use the following process to break down the elements that students need to know, understand, and then do to show mastery of each concept. When analyzing anything, it's better to start with the small picture and move into a larger one; this method will help guide you through that. A great model for standard analysis is Carol

Ann Tomlinson's (2014) Know, Understand, Do (KUD) model. As you see in Table 5.4, a KUD chart is breaking down what a student will need to:

- Know to master the standard
- Understand to master the standard
- Do to show mastery of the standard

Know	Understand	Do
What will a student need to know to master the standard?	What will a student need to understand to master the standard?	What can a student do to show mastery of the standard?

When using each standard, think about all the vocabulary, facts, and information that students need to know to successfully master the standard. Then think about what information they need to understand about the concept to show mastery. These are the big ideas, generalizations, principles, and ideas that transfer across different areas.

Finally, what is the tangible proof of learning? Think about verbs here—what can students do to help them anchor their learning? How do students apply what they have learned to real life?

Those familiar with Bloom's taxonomy will find this model similar to building from lower-order thinking skills to higher-order thinking skills (Bloom, 1970). What do students need to remember, and then what do the students need to understand about this concept to apply, analyze, evaluate, and create? Use Bloom's taxonomy's higher-order skills in the "Do" section. Can students compare, analyze, synthesize, compare, contrast, design, transfer, illustrate, etc.?

Example:

2A—Students cultivate and manage their digital identity and reputation and are aware of the permanence of their actions in the digital world. (ISTE, 2021)

Know	Understand	Do
Positive – how to use technology to interact positively Ethical behavior Interaction Kindness Trolling Triggering	When to keep scrolling: something obviously posted by someone trying to get a response Trolling Triggering subjects and how you can cope	Students are given five mean tweets to rewrite with more appropriate language or content. Then have students post one of the tweets on a classroom discussion board and then respond to each other's tweets appropriately.

The "Know" section looks at information students need to know from the standard. What vocabulary terms can you pull from the standard? Think of this part as the basic information you need to understand the standard. In this standard, the vocabulary terms that students need to know are permanence, digital identity, and reputation.

Then think about what those words connect to as a concept. How do they connect to digital citizenship? When using the terms permanence, digital identity, and reputation, educators commonly use the term "digital footprint." A digital footprint is a cumulative word for permanence, digital identity, and reputation and the concept that students need to understand to master this standard.

For the final part of the analysis, think about:

- What skills are needed to be successful users and members of digital life?

- What is happening at this age developmentally, and how does that correlate to concepts and skills needed for digital life?

- What does it look like when students are interacting with the digital world?

This is the fun part! This is where the lesson is planned. Don't worry about re-creating the wheel; use Bloom's taxonomy verbs to guide your lesson planning (Bloom, 1970). In this standard, the lessons that correlate with the vocabulary and the cumulative concept of digital footprint for a middle-school student are looking at someone's history, looking at the student's name on Google, analyzing non-examples of a digital footprint, setting goals for students' digital footprints, and learning about the filter bubbles they may find themselves in.

⌐ Creation

⌐ first step to building a lesson is to examine the standard. Once the standard ⌐analyzed and you've created a KUD chart (as shown in the previous section), start with the end in mind. What does the student need to do to show mastery of this standard? After the mastery piece is in mind, go back and think about what the student needs to know and understand to show mastery.

Librarians who spent time teaching in the classroom will recognize the name Madelene Hunter. Her seven-step lesson template is the gold standard for lesson creation. It encompasses a clear lesson beginning, middle, and end, with sections for both guided practice and independent practice. When designing digital citizenship lessons for this book, a truncated version of this lesson creation template seems to be most realistic and works best.

Madeleine Hunter's Seven-Step Lesson Template

1. Anticipatory Set

2. Objective and Purpose

3. Teaching and Modeling

4. Guided Practice

5. Check for Understanding

6. Independent Practice

7. Closure (Hunter & Hunter, 2004)

Digital Citizenship Lesson Template

Section	Description
Hook or Anticipatory Set	Show students examples of mean posts about celebrities such as Jimmy Kimmel Live! Mean Tweets. Then explain how users could have reframed their tweet or kept scrolling and not engaged.
Objective/ Purpose	Students learn to protect their digital identity by not responding or creating content impulsively online.
Teaching and Modeling/ Guided Practice	• Explain that even when comments or posts online are triggering, we do not have to respond. • Most of the time it is better to just keep on scrolling, but if you do feel you must respond, take a breath, walk away for an hour, and then type. • Never post while you are feeling a strong emotion, especially if you are upset. • The teacher then models how to edit a mean tweet with more appropriate language.

(Continued)

Section	Description
Independent Practice/ Check for Mastery	Students are given five mean tweets to rewrite with more appropriate language or content. Then have students post one of the tweets on a classroom discussion board and then respond to each other's tweets appropriately.
Materials Needed	A device with Internet access

Starting with the end in mind and referencing the KUD chart that was built for this standard, fill out the section for Independent Practice/Check for Mastery. Now, set the tone for the lesson. How will you hook the students? The word hook in terms of lesson planning is quite literally what a teacher/ librarian will want to do to grab students' attention or pull the students' attention in. What is the anticipatory set that will give them a reason to listen to what is being taught in this lesson? This can be anything from a video clip, a scenario, or an item that would be used in the lesson. Time should be spent planning the hook/anticipatory set, as it will make or break whether this lesson will have students' attention or apathy.

The Objective/Purpose planning piece should allow students to understand the purpose of this lesson. What relevance will this have in their life? For what purpose do they need to learn this skill? Often in classrooms, teachers will post the standard/skill that they are teaching so students have references during the lesson of the objective that they are learning.

Finally, it's time to plan the teaching piece of the lesson. How will all of the things planned come together? What does the teacher/librarian need to say, show, and do during the modeling/guided practice portion of the lesson to make sure students have a clear understanding of the objective and purpose of the lesson? What do they need to know from the teacher/ librarian to complete the independent practice/mastery piece of the lesson? Some teachers/librarians prefer to script out what they will need to say/ do during this part of the lesson plan. Others will find bullet points to be enough to suffice to remind them of the things students need to be taught.

Instruction Delivery

With the KUD process complete, it is time to take that information and decide on the most appropriate methods to support students as they learn. Deciding how to teach digital citizenship topics and skills is challenging even for the most experienced educators. The digital world is in a constant state of flux and reinvention that changes societal norms, processes, and structures, often before there is a chance to adjust from the previous shift.

This affects not only what to teach in digital citizenship but how to teach it. Some questions to consider during this process are:

- How do the concepts or skills from the standard naturally show up in students' lives?

- How do the concepts or skills from the standard inform the way students work through the material?

- How will students access the information and resources they need to master the concepts or skills from the standard?

- How is student agency integral to the mastery of the concepts or skills being taught in the standard?

The overarching thread connecting these questions is context. Teaching concepts and skills outside of their natural context is often reductive and can confuse. Like anything else, students need guided practice *being* digital citizens, not just learning the tenets. The following sections provide specific strategies to consider when preparing how to deliver digital citizenship instruction. This is not an exhaustive list, but is meant as a cognitive model for how to consider the context when deciding the method for delivering instruction.

Asynchronous vs. Synchronous

Start by considering whether there is a need or value in having the lesson be synchronous or asynchronous. Synchronous instruction takes place at a specific time, while asynchronous instruction can be done at any time. For example, a lecture is synchronous if it is watched live either in person or virtually, while a recording of that same lecture is asynchronous because it can be viewed at any time. The unprecedented switch to hybrid instruction during the COVID-19 pandemic made these considerations of time, pace, and place in education standard practice overnight due to the nearly 93 percent of households engaged in some form of distance learning (McElrath, 2020). This dramatic shift in the way students were instructed provided specific benefits for contextualizing digital citizenship instruction and made educators more aware of the nuances of online learning. The answer isn't to make everything digital, but instead, to find digital best practices that specifically benefit student learning.

The benefits of asynchronous instruction are the flexibility of time, pace, and access. It allows learners to access instruction at the point of need both during the time of the lesson and after, and it gives students the freedom to move through the lesson at a pace that matches their fluency. For example, consider asynchronous instruction when covering fundamental skills like password creation because it allows students to access the instruction both during the lesson and when they are creating passwords in real life, and it allows students to go over the content as many times as they need to master the skills. Asynchronous instruction is also helpful when there is a need to provide simultaneous instruction or when a skill can be included in multiple subject areas. The Twitter posting lesson from the last section, for example, would work well asynchronously because appropriate posting is an applicable skill for any academic area, and providing simultaneous access to the lesson allows multiple classes to use it at the same time.

Asynchronous instruction also works well with:

- New vocabulary

- Skill practice

- Technique modeling

- Facts and information

The benefits of synchronous instruction are teacher expertise, collaboration, and resource access. Learning in real time allows teachers to monitor and provide support to students during the lesson, allows students to collaborate and bring their expertise to the lesson, and allows everyone to access resources necessary to specific learning tasks. Synchronous instruction should also be considered based on the learning needs of the students; for example, if student learning benefits from the real-time conversation, group dynamics, or intentional structure.

Content and Subject Integration

The idea of planning and presenting full lessons about digital citizenship can be daunting when thinking of all the other things that are a part of the job description for school librarians. School librarians are unique because they are involved with all departments and subject matters of a campus. Sometimes it is necessary to incorporate digital citizenship standards into existing lessons from other content areas, which would require a librarian to deconstruct digital lesson plans to fit each subject matter's needs.

Deconstruction

Full digital citizenship lessons are taught for depth and complexity, while a deconstructed lesson focuses on the basics of one skill or concept. Think in terms of food. A burger is a fully composed and portioned-out dish. The specific tastes and flavors come in a certain order and are meant to be eaten together because the flavors and textures complement each other. However, there are times when eating a full burger is not possible. This could be for dietary reasons, health benefits, personal preference, or convenience. Deconstructing the burger does not change its basic flavor profile; it just allows it to fit other nutritional needs. In the same way, deconstructing a lesson keeps the essential components while changing to fit the instructional needs of teachers and students. In other words, sometimes a lesson can't just be about digital citizenship; instead find the existing digital citizenship skills within a specific subject or content area. This does not change the integrity of the lesson; it just makes it fit where it's best suited for that subject matter.

Campus-wide Lessons

Campuses often have a set time for school announcements or advisory lessons. These often lend themselves to digital citizenship instruction, but a full lesson at this time may not seem feasible. Using the hook and independent practice is a great way to deconstruct a lesson for whole-campus content creation. On campuses that use Circle Time, a hook can be used as part of the conversation. Practice can be done by breaking into smaller groups. Campuses that use a digital bulletin board/announcement slides can host digital citizenship objectives and purposes. For example, the librarian could create a slide with standard *2B* in mind: *Students engage in positive, safe, legal, and ethical behavior when using technology, including social interactions online or when using networked devices* (ISTE, 2021).

Elementary Lessons

For an elementary-level lesson, you can integrate digital citizenship into themed days. A popular library celebration in public schools centers around Peter Reynold's book *The Dot*. The message of the book is self-expression and creation. Themed days like this are fun for students and teachers and a great way to get students into the library. A center/station menu can guide activities and help spread students out throughout the library. When planning a center/station guide, meet with grade levels/teachers to discuss classroom needs and then incorporate a digital citizenship lesson as part of the centers. The example shown here is for pre-K and kindergarten. It incorporates five skills that kindergarten is addressing in their curriculum and one digital citizenship lesson on a basic level of giving feedback to others through emoji dots. This center helps teach standard *2B—Students engage in positive, safe, legal, and ethical behavior when using technology, including social interactions online or when using networked devices*

INTERNATIONAL DOT DAY
Center / Station Menu

Tear Art Station Fine Motor Skills Use construction paper and a glue stick to fill in a tear art dot.	Twister Name Spelling *Spell your name by walking to your letters *Find the letter that is called
Math Dots Use dot markers to fill in the numbers 1-101	**Digital Citizenship** *EMOJI dots* Find someone's finished tear art, math dots, or dot crown and give them an emoji that shows how you feel about their work. Be positive!
Dot Scavenger Hunt This is a game that involves iPads. Scan QR codes dots around the library to complete each mission	**Dot Crown** Write their names on sentence strips and have them peel dot stickers to place on the letters. Staple together and give them their dot crown.

(ISTE, 2021)—at a basic level of self-expression through commenting/giving feedback.

Elementary school librarians read books aloud as part of their curriculum. Keep the digital citizenship standards handy for those times. In what ways could the book help relate to the standards? Any chance to discuss the standards while students are in front of the librarian is a win for a busy school librarian!

Secondary Lessons

Secondary school librarians can find a way to inject digital citizenship standards and lessons through planning with different subject levels and departments. Librarians' most natural subject integration partner is English language arts (ELA) content, as many digital citizenship standards align with writing and reading standards. When planning with ELA teachers for writing and research, use the digital citizenship standards to enhance or modernize these skills.

Subject Content	Digital Citizenship Content
ELA – Nonfiction	Articles on digital citizenship topics
Math	Math problems – Digital commerce
Government – How laws are made	Digital ethics and laws
Algebra	Algorithms – Filter bubbles, advertising
Social studies – Yellow journalism	Media literacy – Fake news
Research (any subject)	Copyright, fair use
Accounting	Digital commerce – Investing, cryptocurrency
Fine arts	Fair use and Creative Commons
Science	Media literacy

Scheduling the Curriculum

- Permit yourself to have planning time devoted specifically to digital citizenship curriculum planning. Just like classroom teachers are responsible for their content and standards, digital citizenship is the content of the library, and you need to treat it with the validity of a core subject.

- Schedule social media posts a week, a month, or a year in advance. Almost all social media platforms and learning management systems allow users to schedule content to post in the future. Scheduling this in advance will help assure that you stay on target to present information year-round.

- Once you have a curriculum created, immediately start recruiting co-teaching partners and get lessons on the calendar. This provides the accountability to implement rather than getting yourself stuck in the planning process.

- Enlist another librarian from your district or city to go on this journey with you. Having an accountability partner helps ensure that you are sticking to your goals and seeing the digital citizenship curriculum through.

- Share your success at your school, district, or city level! Blast it out on social media; invite local newspapers or community leaders to see what you are doing. Often great ideas and programs end up toiling in obscurity and don't have the effect they should because no one knows about them. Pro-level: Be your PR master and plan your advocacy so that your digital citizenship program doesn't lose steam.

- Make digital citizenship part of your professional goals with your campus or district leadership team. There is a saying that only those things that are measured grow.

Conclusion

Establishing a curriculum is the foundation of creating a digital citizenship culture, and every step of the process is important. Finding or designing scope and sequence establishes the needed context for digital citizenship lessons and provides instruction at the point of need. Analyzing the standards set out by the ISTE focuses lesson planning by ensuring that all the skills and information in the standards are covered in the lesson plan itself (ISTE, 2021). This allows the instruction to be delivered using practices specifically designed to that material, as well as the unique learning needs of the students on your campus.

Taking the time up-front to critically plan how digital citizenship should best be taught in your community is essential to its long-term success. While many are fond of the analogy, "build the plane while it's flying," this approach often leads to one-off lessons that are quickly forgotten by students and never adopted by the campus at large. Rather than limiting creativity and flexibility, a quality plan and curriculum provide the structure librarians need to cultivate collaborative partners that are bought in and that understand the vital role digital citizenship plays in our increasingly digital lives.

CHAPTER 6

School Libraries: Co-teaching and Collaboration with Digital Citizenship

Introduction and Organization

Now that you've laid the groundwork by establishing a digital citizenship curriculum, it's time for implementation. This chapter details how to utilize the practice of co-teaching to better integrate digital citizenship into the instructional practices and programming of your campus or library. This chapter will help you by:

1. Breaking down the co-teaching process for librarians

2. Providing examples of ideal co-teach partnerships

3. Giving suggestions on how to establish yourself as a digital citizenship expert and instructional leader

What Is Co-teaching?

Co-teaching is used in schools to help students benefit from the expertise of two experts in the field. Digital citizenship, in particular, is a multidisciplinary field that benefits from having both a classroom teacher and a librarian touch upon the different elements involved. Co-teaching involves planning and implementation together with both the classroom teacher and the librarian to be most effective. Co-teaching can happen in a classroom or the library; it can be part of extracurricular classes and even used asynchronously. When co-teaching is done perfectly, it blends both teacher and librarian content and skills so seamlessly that students may not even notice where one begins and the other ends.

As a librarian there are three main times that you are called upon to co-teach:

- To help transform or enrich learning (i.e., presentations, author visits, virtual field trips)
- To support literacy
- To teach digital citizenship

In most cases, co-teaching for a librarian involves enhancing or supporting a teacher who is already an expert in a specific area. When co-teaching digital citizenship lessons, the librarian is the expert in the field.

The value of co-teaching in your librarianship practice is that often library lessons are taught out of sync with when students would naturally be using them in their academics. Co-teaching is essential so that those skills are taught to students at the point of need and where they make the most sense in that content area. Teaching digital citizenship concepts out of context does not benefit students long-term. For example, teaching copyright lessons and proprietary digital citizenship lessons works best for students to grasp when they are researching and writing their papers or creating their projects. Students can make a connection between working on something, owning the intellectual property that went into the project/paper, and why someone would care if their work was stolen. They will also be able to immediately begin using the skills of copyright and citation rather than having to recall them from a standalone library lesson taught in the past.

For this book, co-teaching is *mostly* about planning. It would be impossible to physically co-teach every lesson, every day, with every teacher, but it is *not* impossible to plan with teachers in each content area/grade level at least weekly. The main purpose of co-teaching and planning with classroom teachers is that you are embedding digital citizenship content in classroom instruction.

You will have to do the leg work in a professional learning community (PLC) or planning meetings to get buy-in from teachers before you can implement digital citizenship lessons concurrently. Remember, digital citizenship is often seen as your agenda at first; teachers may not see the value in it as it applies to their curriculum until they see how it blends into their curriculum. They have to see that it does not add one more thing to their plate; instead, it makes their curriculum more contextual and real-world. For example, secondary math classes are a great place to incorporate media literacy skills because the skills being taught in classes such as algebra or statistics are directly applicable to analyzing infographics, statistics, or e-commerce purchases. A simple way to do this is to create a series of quick warm-up math problems that utilize current stats or graphics. This covers both the math standards and digital citizenship skills.

As you build trust and relationships, come to planning meetings and PLCs with ideas of your own to add to the lessons you're planning. You are building a culture of trust and digital citizenship simultaneously.

Co-teaching Strategies and Practices

There are several different levels of involvement for a librarian to be seen as a co-teacher. The table below provides an overview of some of the common ways that librarians are involved as co-teachers. We name and describe each type, provide a rough estimate of the workload division, and share when to best utilize it to cover content. Following the table is a more in-depth description of each co-teaching type, as well as real-world examples of when we have utilized this type of co-teaching in our own library programs. The purpose here is to broaden the concept of co-teaching and help you consider different approaches that better meet the needs of students and teachers.

TYPES OF CO-TEACHING

Type of Co-teaching	Instructional Division	Description	Best Used When
You're In Charge	70% librarian 30% instructional partner	• Librarian delivers and models most of the lesson, while the instructional partner takes on more of a supporting role by helping individual students and answering more content-specific questions.	• Skills and topics students need to master are not content-specific, like digital citizenship.
Your Turn My Turn	50% librarian 50% instructional partner	• Both the librarian and instructional partner evenly split the lesson responsibilities by presenting, supporting, and modeling at equal levels.	• Librarian has a comfort level of content being taught. • Content is interdisciplinary. • Lessons span several class periods.

(Continued)

(Continued)

Type of Co-teaching	Instructional Division	Description	Best Used When
			• Librarians are helping teach an entire unit.
Gradual Release	Starts with "You're in Charge" and gradually becomes instructional partner–led only	• Librarian models lesson for a classroom teacher and then gradually releases teaching to instructional partner. • Primary schools and younger grade levels: co-teaching spans several days with the librarian helping more at the beginning of the week and tapering off toward the end of the week. In primary grades, this may take place over several days, with the librarian helping the teacher more at the beginning of the week, and tapering off as the week progresses. • Secondary schools and upper-grade levels: the librarian may teach the first few periods of the day with minimal support from the classroom teacher and as the day progresses, the roles flip, and the librarian is supporting the classroom teacher as the teacher is the main presenter.	• Librarian co-teaches with an entire grade level or department. • The librarian is coaching a teacher through a specific skill set.
Instructional Support	30% librarian 70% instructional partner	• Librarian aids instructional partner with technology support or assistance during teaching and helps plan lesson.	• The teacher wants to implement technology that may have seemed intimidating to them on their own.

(Continued)

(Continued)

Type of Co-teaching	Instructional Division	Description	Best Used When
			• A teacher is willing to try new things and needs help implementing technology in a lesson.
Preloading	10% librarian 90% instructional partner	• This allows the teacher to be the main presenter during the lesson as the teacher explains the project/paper guidelines and then supports students as the librarian teaches.	• The librarian needs to explain where students will get the information needed for an assignment. • This approach is best used when a teacher is assigning a project that involves students relying on sources other than the teacher for information.
Making Resources	10% librarian 90% instructional partner	• Involves the librarian being more involved with making the material for the assignment rather than presenting the information to students.	• Teachers are looking to liven up a lesson with technology or new resources.

Your Turn My Turn (50%)

This is the most common style of co-teaching, where the librarian and teacher evenly split the lesson responsibilities. Both are presenting, supporting, and modeling at equal levels. This benefits teachers because the lesson can be more complex and often go deeper because two professionals are making and crafting the content. This benefits students because you are better able to differentiate learning and support the individual needs of students. It helps with classroom management. Pacing is better because the student-to-teacher ratio is smaller. This is a great approach once you've reached a comfort level with the content and teacher. This is also helpful when the content is interdisciplinary. This can be particularly beneficial when the content spans several class periods or when you are helping teach an entire unit.

Project-based learning is a great time for the 50/50 co-teach strategy, especially when embedding digital citizenship skills and topics, because to be successful in project-based learning, students have to utilize skills outside of the content standards for that class. One of my favorite projects is with our dance class. Each year they have to create their choreography based on the style of a famous dancer. This requires media literacy skills, musical copyright skills, research skills from both databases and online sources, and video editing and online posting rules because they post the videos on YouTube, and they have to understand fair use and creative ownership. These are all skills that are outside of those included in the standards for that class.

Librarian-Heavy Co-teaching

You're in Charge (70%–30%)

In this form of co-teaching, the librarian is doing the main lesson delivery and skill modeling. The teacher takes on more of a supporting role by helping individual students and answering more content-specific questions. This is a beneficial style because it gives the teacher more freedom to coach students, allows digital citizenship to be the focus, and helps librarians build an academic relationship with students. This is a good approach to consider when the skills and topics students need to master are not content-specific like digital citizenship.

I find this co-teaching style works well with content like math and science where the content standards and digital citizenship standards do not have as much overlap. A great example of this is a renewable energy unit I've taught with our Environments Science classes. I teach about fair use, resource evaluation, and infographic creation, and the teacher walks the room making sure the students understand what renewable energy is, the different types, etc. The focus of the lesson is the digital citizenship skills, so I as the expert am guiding the learning. However, the students are using the digital citizenship skills to show mastery of their renewable energy standards, so the teacher needs to be active in the lesson to ensure that this is happening

Gradual Release

This form of co-teaching is a way for the librarian to model lessons for a classroom teacher. In primary schools, this may take place over several days, with the librarian helping the teacher more at the beginning of the week and tapering off as the week progresses, with the classroom teacher becoming the main presenter. In secondary schools, a librarian may teach the first few periods of the day with minimal support from the classroom teacher. As the day progresses, the roles flip, and the librarian is supporting the classroom teacher, as the teacher is the main presenter. Often this form of co-teaching allows a librarian to leave the teacher halfway through the day or week. The benefits of this approach are that the librarian can reach more students, and it lets the librarian instill digital citizenship practices in teachers. This is a good approach to consider when the librarian is co-teaching with an entire grade level or department, as it allows them to spend time with every teacher. It is also a good strategy for coaching teachers to develop their digital citizenship skills.

This method works well with subjects that have several areas of overlap with digital citizenship standards such as language classes, social studies, and career and technology classes. I often use this method when covering topics like media literacy with English co-teachers because after a few times of seeing me teach the material, they have mastered the skill or content. Sometimes I don't even have to go to their classes. The teacher will simply come to the library to plan, and I'll model the skills and help create the resources for the lesson. Then they go and teach the digital citizenship content. While this is more like co-planning or coaching versus co-teaching, the students are still getting the benefit of my digital citizenship expertise, so I think it counts! Also, there is only one of me and over 2,000 students at my campus, and I cannot physically co-teach with every teacher and subject. If I have any hope of making an impact on students' digital citizenship knowledge and skills, I need to coach up other digital citizenship experts on campus.

Teacher-Heavy Co-teaching
Tech Support (70%–30%)

Sometimes librarians are asked to co-teach because a teacher needs technology support or assistance during teaching. This type of co-teaching often requires the librarian to spend more time during the planning phase to build a lesson using technology with the teacher. There is less time for the librarian in front of students teaching the material. The librarian is still part of the lesson but is usually there to explain how to use the technology and assist students with specific questions about the technology. The benefits of this approach to co-teaching are that it allows the teacher to implement technology that may have seemed intimidating to them on their own, and it exposes students to new ways to show learning. Technology support co-teaching is a great approach to consider for a strong content teacher who may desire to use technology but doesn't have the comfort level with it. It is also great to use for a teacher who is willing to try new things and needs help implementing technology in a lesson.

One of my favorite technology lessons to teach is using Google Slides to make stop-motion videos. I've used this with English, health, and history. Students can tell a story using Google Slides based on the information that the teacher wants them to incorporate and then animate the slides to make a video they send to the teacher. As the librarian, I need almost no information about the content for this type of co-teaching. It usually helps if I know what the project requirements are so I can help students who are making slides know what they need to incorporate. This requires me to address students as a class at the beginning of the lesson to explain how to make the stop-motion videos and then help them individually on an as-needed basis.

Making Resources (90%–10%)

This form of co-teaching involves the librarian being more involved with making the material for the assignment rather than presenting the information to students. This could be helping to build a slideshow, curating databases or resources, or making or curating video tutorials for students. This benefits the teacher because they are free to focus on the content and provide students with a deeper understanding of the assignment. Students are given curated resources, templates, or material to use for their project from an expert that will help them with their projects. This is a great approach to consider for teachers who are looking to liven up a lesson with technology or new resources.

I was able to help eighth-grade students make light of their experience with video conferencing classes due to the pandemic by building a lesson that required them to make video conferences of characters in a book they were reading for an English assignment. The assignment was to retell the story, evaluate character traits, and show their understanding of the novel. As the librarian, I built a template in Google Slides that looked like Google Meet (the video conferencing software that my district used during the pandemic shutdown) for them to put character pictures on a screen and then used the present and chat feature to allow students to retell the story. My job as co-teacher was to show them how to add images and text and use the template I built—which most students innately understood. I was not able to make it to all the classes in the department who wanted to do this project, so I made a video and sent it to teachers to place in their students' Google Classrooms. The results were fantastic, as students showed their savvy with how a video conference call goes!

Preloading (90%–10%)

When teachers assign projects or research papers, they often need librarians to front-load the students with basic information about digital citizenship, citing work, using databases or resources, or knowing where to find information. This allows the librarian to be the main presenter during the lesson as the teacher explains the project/paper guidelines and then supports students as the librarian teaches. These benefit teachers by allowing the librarian to explain where students will get the information needed for an assignment. This approach is best used when a teacher is assigning a project that involves students relying on sources other than the teacher for information.

I have been able to use this approach often in helping history teachers jump-start National History Day projects. Students need to know information about questioning, research, theme, resources to use, how to cite information, where to get images and videos they can use, and how to use technology to build projects, which are all part of the librarian wheelhouse. Once they are presented with that information, the teacher can help them hone their interests into projects and research further, but the information about how to do the project and where to find information come from me in the preloading session!

Instructional Leadership in Digital Citizenship

It is important to see yourself, a school librarian, as a campus leader because you are the only one on campus (in most cases) who does the role you do. If you are not a part of your campus leadership team, now is the time to become part of it! Campus leadership teams usually consist of administration, counselors, department heads/grade-level chairs, and instructional coaches. Many campuses view the librarian as part of that leadership team, but if you find yourself on a campus that doesn't, offer to present to your campus leadership team specifically about digital citizenship so that they can see the value of what you do in the library and beyond. Make sure your administrators know of your desire to be part of the leadership team so that you are included. Your expertise in digital citizenship will prove valuable once they understand what you can help the students and staff do.

Here are a few ideas to start building your clout as a digital citizenship expert and establish yourself as a campus leader:

- Offer professional development lessons on digital citizenship topics and skills.

Consider not only campus-level training but also district professional development sessions. Schedule several opportunities to attend, including before, during, or after school. Providing asynchronous training may also boost attendance and completion because teachers and staff can work on it at their own pace. This can be as simple as hanging informational flyers in the teachers' lounge, sending out newsletters and video tutorials via email, or creating full-on lessons with continuing education hours. The key is to provide as much choice as possible because, just like students, adult learners engage more when they have a say in their learning.

- Volunteer to coach or mentor new teachers on campus.

Supporting new teachers not only gives them the benefit of your teaching expertise but also gives you a unique opportunity to instill them with digital citizenship knowledge. Don't assume that younger teachers know about or have more information about digital citizenship than you. Younger teachers need this information too, sometimes at a more serious level. While they tend to be more comfortable with technology, they may not have the skills to be a good digital citizen when using it.

- Use campus/district initiatives that are already being required to embed digital citizenship information.

My district used the Sandy Hook Promise, Say Something curriculum a few years ago. I was in charge of implementing the initiative on our campus, which I did through a series of lessons through our daily announcements and some asynchronous lessons sent to teachers. The information in this curriculum lent itself to many digital citizenship conversations, and I implemented lessons and discussion questions on digital citizenship through what was being required with Say Something.

- Embed digital citizenship into things you're already doing as the librarian or for the campus.

Think through all the other things that are asked of you daily. Are you asked to help with daily announcements? Do you help run your campus social media? How can you use duties assigned to you to incorporate digital citizenship? I always ask to be part of our school social media on campus because it allows me to disseminate information about what is happening in our school library to all stakeholders. I also help with daily announcements because it allows me to reach all students with information about the library. Since I'm already doing these duties, I use my access to them to share information about being safe online and how to be a good digital citizen.

- Share digital citizenship skills and topics at subject/grade-level planning meetings.

Ask the person in charge of the planning meeting if you can share a quick digital citizenship presentation with the group. Most planning meetings are tightly structured, and they have a ton of content to cover, so keep it brief and specifically target the topics to skills related to the group. If you are not sure what topics would be a good fit, check out the table on page 99 for some quick ideas.

Co-teaching can be whatever you make it. If you've never done it before, start small. Choose one subject/grade level to plan with and throw yourself into it from there.

Subject Content	Digital Citizenship Content
English language arts – Nonfiction	Articles on digital citizenship topics
Math	Digital commerce
Government	Digital ethics and digital law
Social Studies – Yellow journalism	Media literacy – Fake news
Research (any subject)	Copyright, fair use
Accounting/business/financial literacy	Digital commerce – investing, cryptocurrency
Fine arts	Fair use and creative commons
Science	Media literacy

Building Co-teach Partnerships

There are a few different ways to approach co-teaching. The first thing to do is to set an attainable goal. A co-teaching goal sheet may include some or all of the following goals.

Once you have set goals for co-teaching, use one or more of the following strategies to build co-teaching partnerships. You may need to start outside of digital citizenship.

Strategies for Getting Your Foot in the Door

Preparation

- Read the curriculum of a grade level/department you're interested in co-teaching with.

  This will allow you to approach them with ideas. Saying, "I noticed you're going to be working on _____; I have an idea for a lesson we could do together," makes you accessible.

- Get advice on teachers to target.

  Talk to coaches, administration, or department heads/lead teachers about your desire to co-teach and ask who you could benefit from the most.

- Ask for planning schedules from all departments and grade levels and show up at planning meetings!

  If you are unable to physically show up in meetings, use video conferencing to attend virtually. You could also invite the department or grade level to your space in the library to plan. If you need to leave the library to attend meetings, make a plan for your library to be attended by another teacher or office staff member. If you have student library helpers, make plans to have them go to a supervised office or classroom while you're gone or have someone sit with them in the library while you're in planning so that the library is still open and accessible to students who want to check books in or out.

- Look for subjects that lend themselves to a more fluid schedule.

  Some classes to consider are yearbook, art, theater, or really any elective or extracurricular activity. In other words, seek out the teachers who teach nontested subjects/classes.

- Look for hot topics that interest campus teachers and include them in marketing to attract them.

  This can be anything from what is going on in your community or campus to national news. A great example of a hot topic recently has been fake news. Librarians have been able to appeal to teachers because of their expertise in verified sources.

- Step out of your comfort zone.

When I taught fourth and sixth grade, I taught what most elementary school teachers refer to as upper grades, fourth and sixth. When I became an elementary school librarian, I was suddenly thrust into the world of what is commonly called the lower or younger grades (pre-kindergarten through second or third grade). I did not have the experience with them in the classroom, so naturally, I had a lower comfort level teaching them as a librarian. At the time, my district was focusing closely on making sure that students were reading on grade level by third grade. I knew that I could enhance my library program to help my campus meet the goals of the district, but it would involve me diving headfirst into a group of teachers and students that I didn't know as much about as I would like. I approached the four kindergarten teachers on my campus and discussed my desire to involve myself with them more. They were excited to have me as a planning partner. I didn't take over in planning; I offered my space in the library and my time as a co-teacher. We were able to plan some amazing lessons and some enriching activities together that satisfied the needs of the teachers and students in that grade level and let me get involved with the students and teachers. When we planned centers especially, they were always eager to let me include something with technology, and that often allowed me to speak to students about digital citizenship. I met with them twice weekly after school to plan with them. I learned so much that year and connected with the students and teachers in that grade level. This was a huge leap from my sixth-grade teaching days, but I loved it. *What is your comfort zone, and how can you step out of it this year to enhance your library program?*

Strategies for Marketing

- Service menus.

  Make menus of services or lessons that you can help teachers with and send them out in email or post in common areas.

  Service menus worked especially well for me as an elementary school librarian. A flexible schedule in the library in elementary school leaves some classroom teachers concerned they won't be utilizing the library with their students. A service menu is a good thing for teachers to have a point of reference during planning so that they can see how they can be involved in the library. Then I offered sign-up times along with a service menu and let teachers find times that best fit what they needed to come to the library. In middle school and high school, I have presented during the first-of-the-year professional development with a list of things I can do or help teach so that teachers are aware of me as a resource.

- Yelp yourself!

  Once you finish co-teaching, have teachers give you positive reviews you can share with others. Include those reviews in other marketing you do for the library.

  Social media is a great place to share stories about successful co-teach collaborations. Tag teachers when you do this and invite them to like, share, and comment! Additionally, make sure you tag your campus social media account as well and ask them to interact with the post. (This is particularly easy if you are also in charge of the campus social media accounts!) For more information about using social media internally at your library or campus, see Chapter 3.

- Bathrooms.

  Never underestimate the power of a flyer on a bathroom stall. Use that blank space to advertise your services.

  Bathroom flyers are a great way to drive traffic to asynchronous lessons or resources you've developed. Many teachers on our campus had expressed a desire to incorporate resource evaluation skills into their content, So we created a fake news digital breakout using Google Forms that could be included in any subject area. To spread the word, we designed a flyer with a QR code advertising the resource and posted it in all of the teacher bathrooms. It was a great success!

- Newsletters.

  Set a goal to send out newsletters to your staff that include all the ways you can be a valuable resource on campus

When schools were forced to shut down due to the COVID-19 pandemic, I started curating a frequently-asked-question list to keep track of the questions I was being asked as the librarian by teachers. I turned it into a newsletter with questions as topics and provided weekly newsletters. I loved having this curated information available to teachers, so I continued writing newsletters this past school year. Archived newsletters are great to be able to quickly send to teachers who have questions that a previous newsletter addressed.

Strategies for Building Relationships

- Get involved in other school activities.

  Sometimes you can build partnerships with teachers by attending games, helping volunteer on committees, becoming part of parent–teacher associations (PTAs), or other organizations on campus.

One of my favorite committees to become involved in on-campus is the Sunshine Committee. In my district, the Sunshine Committee is the party-planning committee of the school. We plan baby and wedding showers, special events, and ways to boost teacher morale. I love being part of this committee because people always want to be where a party is, so I meet and build relationships through time spent with people, and it allows me to be associated with a good time or positivity.

- Look for teachers who are willing.

  Most of the time there are people on campus who are in charge of other things beyond their classroom. Those individuals may be willing to let you in because they could use any help they can get. Look for people like coaches, new teachers, teachers who teach elective classes on top of core content, English as a second language (ESL) teachers, or teachers who mentor on campus and offer to help them in any way you can.

I have found that athletic coaches are great candidates for co-teaching. They already understand the benefits of teamwork and naturally understand how to divide responsibilities. Plus, they always have so much on their plate that they welcome your support and help.

- Show your teachers love.

  The power of a positive handwritten note goes a long way. Stand in the hallway during passing periods to greet and talk with them. Offer a listening ear, support them any way you can, and if all else fails, a piece of chocolate is an act of love on a school campus!

I once worked for a wonderful principal who had everyone in leadership meetings write a handwritten note to someone that they saw being exceptional that week. I loved this practice for two reasons:

1. It allowed me to look for positives all week—I sought out stories of teachers going above and beyond
2. It always had the best response from the person who received the note. I have never written a note that the recipient didn't come down to the library and thank me for my kind words or for noticing what they were doing. I also loved when I would go into classrooms and see the notes I had written to teachers hanging up on their walls or desk. It's a simple act, but it has a powerful outcome.

- Offer technology assistance.

  This simple act of offering to assist a teacher with technology opens doors. It allows them to trust and think of you as someone they can go to for help. Use that foundation to build a relationship and co-teaching partnership.

Both as a librarian and as an instructional technology coach, I have found there is no better way to build trust with a teacher or coworker than to fix their projector. Or their printer. Or their smartboard. If they can't count on you for the small things, they will never trust you when their job is on the line, which for teachers of tested subjects is not hyperbolic. The key is to talk about instructional ideas or co-teach possibilities while you are fixing the printer. Ask: what they are teaching? What are they using the smartboard for that day? Also, ask them how their day is going. Be a person. This strategy has never failed me. Not once.

- Look for small ways to build trust.

  How can you be of help to teachers on your campus in a way that builds a foundation of trust? Any small act of kindness or assistance is a way to begin a relationship.

At the beginning of the year, I always try to make a small presentation during professional development that tells teachers things I can do to help them. This has always proven to be a great way to meet new teachers because they are always in need of some help setting up technology or just figuring out how the campus works. Letting them know that I'm there for small or large things is a great way to extend a helping hand. Then I make a point of following through with helping them when they ask for it.

- Re-word no.

  Instead of telling teachers no, use phrases like "I can't right now" or "I don't know but I'll find out." Instead of being a dead end, become a bridge or a highway.

  The fastest way to turn people off is to tell them no. I work very hard to avoid barriers in my library. Simply re-wording "no" answers has helped me accomplish this.

I have learned that when I help people do some digging to find answers, it improves my ability to serve because I now know more things than I did before they asked me! If I can't do something when someone needs me, I answer with, "I can't right now, but is there another time that works today/this week?" This gives people the mindset that you are not telling them no—you are not a wall that they encounter in the library, but a person who is busy but makes sure they know they are valued and important as well.

- Assist teachers who are in charge of competitions.

  Become involved with teachers who have students that compete in state-level or national competitions like National History Day, Destination Imagination, Advanced Placement, debate, and Academic Decathlon (ACADECA). Offer assistance and library space to host practices, displays, etc.

Volunteering to help with academic competitions and events is a great way to showcase your talents as an educator and prove that you are a reliable partner. During my first year at my school, I volunteered as a competition judge and helped facilitate Saturday math tutoring sessions. This established my credibility with the math and history department heads, who helped run those events. From then on they trusted me to collaborate with their teachers, which in turn provided me with the opportunity to incorporate digital citizenship into those lessons.

Strategies for Using Your Resources

- Set up a space where teachers can collaborate so they feel welcome. This allows teachers to plan near you and allows you to give input while they're there.

We recently transformed our old library office into a conference room/collaboration space. Our high school campus is large (it is a quarter-mile from one side to the other), and it was difficult for my partner librarian and me to consistently attend planning meetings. We provided a space in the library for teacher planning, and now they come to us. Creating a conference room is also helpful for student workers who can't be unattended.

- Offer to host baby or wedding showers or other fun activities for teachers in the library.

    This gives you a chance to get them in the library and work magic from there.

> Hosting teacher events after or during school is one of my favorite things because I like to party, plan, and host events. Even if you don't like those things, offering your space for these kinds of events has people from all over the building coming to you. When they're in your space, they're more likely to see something that sparks interest or talk to you. This is a great way to mingle with teachers in subject areas you may not typically co-teach with and build relationships outside of your same circle. It also lets teachers feel the vibe of the library, and they'll want to be back with their class. Getting teachers to your space and in front of you is often half the battle; when there are cupcakes and punch involved, you'll have them all running!

- Offer your space.

    Sometimes teachers need a change of scenery. Offer your space during the school day, but also for tutoring or after-school events.

> One of my favorite pre-pandemic events was something I called "Full House Fridays" in the library. It was a chance for teachers to bring classes down to the library, spread out, and let students work on their own in a different space than the classroom. I was lucky enough to have room for about four classes of 25 kids in my middle-school library, so Full House Fridays was just that! I started this by inviting the social studies team down to finish projects I had done with them and then I posted a picture to Twitter calling it a Full House Friday—the next week I had the English department wanting to take part in the same activity. Beyond Full House Friday, I made sure that the library space was available in an open invitation for teachers to help students before or after school or even if students needed a break from the classroom just to finish an assignment or some social emotional learning (SEL) time. There is never a point when I say the space is off limits.

What Do You Do When You Attend a PLC or Other Co-teach Planning Session?

Before

- Know something.

    If you have time, read up on the curriculum of the grade level or department that you're attending the PLC of. If you are not able to do that, it's good to go in at least knowing what they're doing in class, even if you just know the topic.

- Bring a cheat sheet.

  Come prepared with your state, district, or other standards for librarians and your campus or district library mission and vision. If you have those things on hand, you'll be able to reference them as they talk and see how you can bring your role into their planning.

- Have some asynchronous lessons ready to offer.

  Make a playlist of all your video tutorials or lessons and have them ready to click and send if they are interested.

- Know your resources.

  What can your library offer to enhance lessons? What physical or digital resources can you offer? Does your district offer virtual reality (VR) goggles? What about picture books?

- Build an online portfolio.

  This is how you know you've achieved expert level. Build a website of everything you can offer and examples of past lessons or collaborations with other teachers or grade levels.

- Find out what projects or research papers are coming up.

  What can you offer to help with during those times?

- Respect their time.

  Be on time, use their time to plan, stay on task, and then thank them for their time.

- Don't come with a personal agenda.

  An agenda in a meeting is good—a personal agenda is not!

- Don't have expectations for how you think the meeting should go.

  Instead, say things like "I am here to be a resource while you are planning."

- Create a planning template.

  Prepare questions so that you can capture all the important points.

During (Go in with the Following Mindset):

- Go in actively showing you're ready.

  Bring your computer, notepad, and calendar, and be ready for anything.

- Don't be afraid to give little to no input.

  The first couple of times you may not have anything to say, and honestly, you may just need to feel out the group. If they see you, they're more likely to think about how they can use you, so just your presence is enough.

- Be positive.

  Find something to compliment in their planning and let them know you're on their side.

- Ask about concerns and struggles.

  Which concept in this unit are students or teachers struggling with the most? What can you offer to help?

- Think possible.

  Where teachers may feel overwhelmed by a concept or assignment, think about how you can make it possible in the time and the constraints that you have.

- Seek to understand.

  Listen to what teachers are talking about and where they have apprehension or struggles. Work to understand their teaching style and what they're most comfortable with.

- Ask for deadlines so you can plan accordingly.

- Always clarify expectations before the meeting ends.

  Make sure you understand what they want from you and what is expected from students in the lessons.

- Think smaller.

  Don't feel like everything you offer to do has to be a full lesson or experience in the library. Offer services where you can. Do teachers need help with bell ringers or warm-ups? Would a video tutorial on a new website or app benefit them?

- Reteach.

  When teachers are having to reteach concepts, how can you help them rework the information?

- Don't tell people what to do.

  Instead, make suggestions.

- Don't compare.

  Offer examples of what other teachers or schools have done with certain topics, projects, etc., but don't make it appear that you're comparing the PLC you're in to another.

- Avoid drama and school politics.

  Don't participate in these discussions during PLCs. Help steer the conversation back on topic if you need to.

- Don't pretend to know more than you do.

  Saying "I don't know, but I'll find out" is less harmful than pretending to know!

- Don't push your needs first.

  Instead of saying what you are there to do, listen to what they are talking about and offer input on how you could help.

- Don't criticize.

  Always assume positive intent. For the most part, teachers are professionals with great care for students and a desire to be successful. They may not do things the way you would, but find the positive instead of criticizing them to their face or behind their back.

- Don't talk the whole time.

  As you know, time is a commodity on a school campus; don't take up valuable PLC time by talking the whole time.

- Don't tune out.

  Don't give the appearance of tuning out. Stay off your phone or device. Be present and active in the conversation; even a nodding head is better than a blank stare.

After

- Thank them.
- Open communication.
- You don't have to go to every meeting every time, but make sure they know they can reach out to you at any time.
- Set up your next appointment immediately.
- Follow through.

  Don't say you'll do something or offer to be part of lessons and then not show up or have your part prepared.

- Don't overbook yourself.

  Booking activities, lessons, and time in the library is our favorite thing as librarians. Just give yourself time to prepare for lessons accordingly.

Follow Up after the Co-Teach Lesson(s)

- When done with an initial co-teaching experience, follow up with the PLC or teacher and ask:

  - *What worked?*

  - *What didn't?*

  - *What could be done differently?*

  - *When can we meet again?*

  - *What are some things you noticed you could do better or differently?*

Finally, *share*. Advocate for your library program by letting all stakeholders know what you did. Share photos on social media that explain what students did with the librarian today. Have a section in your newsletter where a teacher can talk about co-teaching experience. They don't know what you're doing unless you tell them or show them.

Recommendations for Instructional Partner Collaborations

As your digital citizenship program starts to grow, you will need to recruit other experts and campus personnel to help grow your reach and add value. Some partners are more obvious, such as department heads/lead teachers/grade-level chairs, because they are intimately involved with the library in general. But don't count out other members of the school campus and the impact they can have on building a digital citizenship culture.

Support Staff

For the purpose of this chapter, the support staff is anyone on campus that isn't in the classroom but is responsible for leading both students and teachers/staff members. These staff members are more flexible in their schedules and more specialized in their job on campus. These specializations can bring a different perspective to digital citizenship and can make you aware of specific needs or trending issues on your campus.

- Technology coaches.

  There is some overlap with librarians and technology coaches or instructional technology coaches. Technology coaches can be a great partner for a librarian, who can at times be an island on campus. Use this person on campus as your digital citizenship partner to help craft meaningful and targeted lessons on digital citizenship.

- School counselors and psychologists.

    These professionals often deal with social-emotional issues of students on campus. They will be in tune with what issues students on the campus are facing, specifically regarding technology (cyberbullying, hacking student accounts, cries for help, etc.). Counselors are also able to help the librarian use social-emotional ideas to intertwine with digital citizenship.

- At-risk coordinators.

    These people on campus are often privy to details about students that can hinder or prevent them from being successful in school. Find ways you can work with them to help target groups or provide specific lessons and training to fill gaps both interpersonal and academic.

- Administrative team.

    Once you have these folks on your team, you'll never look back. They will provide information about teachers who need specific help with instruction or digital classroom management that deals specifically with technology. They can also help with general information about problems with students arising on campus due to technology or digital citizenship.

- After-school staff.

    If your school runs programs after school, these professionals can be a great asset for school-wide initiatives. They have more flexibility in teaching and are often looking for better relationships with the school staff. They also have regular outside presenters, instructors, and others come into their program.

Curriculum Staff

- Instructional specialists.

    Instructional specialists or coaches can give information about the curriculum as a standards expert and could help you integrate digital citizenship lessons. Having this background information from an instructional specialist will help when you go to planning or PLC meetings with departments/grade levels.

- Department heads/lead teachers/grade-level chairs.

    These are the professionals who are running the PLCs/departments/ grade levels on campus. They often have insight into what teachers in that area are doing well or need help with. As leaders on campus, these people are often responsible for the instructional focus and pedagogical approach of the department/subject area/grade level. They can also act as gatekeepers. Once you win their trust, you are in. If the department head is working with you, then you earn credibility and clout with the other teachers in that area.

Community Stakeholders

- Public librarians.

  Get to know the public librarians in your school district or area. Involve them in initiatives or digital citizenship focuses. Public librarians are also great at letting you know what is going on in your community. How can you be involved with helping your students become public library patrons? Use this relationship like a bridge to help students, specifically at-risk students who may not have Internet or use technology at home, to use the library for those purposes. Public librarians are also able to help inform parents about digital citizenship, which trickles down to the students on your campus.

- Businesses.

  Get business owners or managers involved in your campus by asking them to come talk about digital citizenship and how it applies in their field. These partnerships can also help your students understand why good digital citizenship is important to people hiring for jobs.

- Parents.

  Get involved with parents on your campus! This will help in two ways: giving you information about what their needs are and helping co-support their child's digital citizenship development. Present at PTAs, meet with booster clubs, meet with prom planning committees, etc., or send out a survey asking what parents need information about in terms of digital citizenship. Find parent experts who could present on different digital citizenship topics.

Other Opportunities to Create a Digital Citizenship Culture on Campus

- Announcements.

  Any time you can use your school's bulletin board, rolling announcements, daily announcements, or marquee, find a way to incorporate digital citizenship content.

- Social media posts.

  At the beginning of the year, preschedule four posts on the social media platforms for your campus and library. This can include digital citizenship practices, articles, video tutorials, or skill reminders. Use the scope and sequence to time the posts based on that month's element or standard.

- Professional development.

  Plan synchronous and asynchronous professional development for your campus. Go a step further and see if you can present on a district level in your district's continuing education offerings.

- Library programming (library design challenges).

  Kill two birds with one stone by offering fun library challenges or programs that incorporate digital citizenship ideas.

- Community education.

  Reach out to recreation centers, public libraries, community colleges, nonprofits, women's shelters, home school groups, and other community organizations in your area to offer digital citizenship presentations, or just provide posters that you make with information about digital citizenship.

Conclusion

Establishing and maintaining a digital citizenship culture is not done in isolation; it takes a community. Collaborate, co-teach, and communicate with those in your school and community, and they will begin to understand why digital citizenship skills are essential to the success of our culture and society. The content and skills of digital citizenship are rooted in every aspect of life and require a multidisciplinary approach to effectively address this complexity. Cryptocurrency, nano-influencer marketing, digital ownership, telemedicine, misinformation, nonfungible tokens (NFTs), privacy rights, and esports are just a few of the trending topics in our world right now, and expecting yourself to be the expert in all of these areas is naive at best and hubris at worst. You are an information professional. Do some research, seek out experts, and let them help. It's dangerous to go alone. Bring friends!

CHAPTER 7

Startup Lessons

This section includes 18 lesson plans for six different digital citizenship elements. We call them startup lessons because they are designed to help librarians and teachers get started planning their first digital citizenship lessons. Since every library, school, and situation are unique, the lessons are intentionally only planned out at the concept level. This also helps keep the lessons as relevant as possible, because technology and the culture it serves change so rapidly. Our goal is that you can take these lessons, add your spin to them, and help make them relevant to the students you serve.

Each digital citizenship element has three corresponding lesson plans: one for elementary, one for middle school, and one for high school. All the lessons are vertically aligned to show what concepts of each element can be taught at each age level. There is also a corresponding International Society of Educational Technology (ISTE) standard for each lesson. Sometimes this remains the same across all three lessons, but sometimes it changes because the complexity of the concept is aligned more to a different standard.

We further broke down the lessons into full lessons, short lessons, warm-ups, and social media/announcement posts. The purpose of this is to demonstrate how to teach digital citizenship in any space, at any time, and across all communication channels at school or in your community. No matter how big or small the stage, there is a way to share digital citizenship content. We also included ideas for co-teaching partnerships, some specific resources to help support the lesson, and (if appropriate) an asynchronous version of the lesson.

‑Up Lesson Plan Layout

Following is a detailed explanation of each part of the lesson plan. It includes what each part is and how to use it to finish planning out the lesson.

Lesson Title—A fun title idea for the lesson!

Digital Citizenship Element—The element covered in the lesson.

ISTE Standard—The ISTE standard aligns with the digital citizenship element above.

Full Lesson—To outline the full lesson, we used the modified Madeline Hunter model from Chapter 5.

Section	Description
Hook or Anticipatory Set	When creating the hooks, we intentionally chose experiential activities wherever possible, such as games, read-aloud, etc. Digital citizenship lessons aren't necessarily technology-heavy, so it is nice to give students a chance.
Objective/ Purpose	The objective or purpose is always written as a "Students will" statement to keep it actionable and observable. We also did this in case your school requires that the objective is posted in the room.
Teaching and Modeling/ Guided Practice	This section of the lesson is often broad. While we do provide specific points to highlight or cover, we don't say how you have to cover them. You could use a slide deck, make a tutorial video, make an escape room, etc. This is also the section that will need to be updated with the latest data or technology. If there is a specific skill to practice, we provide an activity or teacher modeling suggestion.
Independent Practice/ Check for Mastery	A great way to show mastery of a topic or skill is to create with it, so often the independent practice we recommend is a project or activity. While these can be done as a group, all of them work as individual assignments.
Materials Needed	We tried not to require too many materials for the lessons, especially in the upper grades. Mostly, students just need a device with access to the Internet. This could even be their phone in most instances.

Co-teaching Suggestions

Here we list any class, subject, or content that would fit well with the content of the lesson. This might be an overall subject like English or a specific skill in that subject like persuasive writing. Finally, we provide suggestions for slight alterations to the lesson that would help it fit another subject. For example, focusing on medical influencers in a science class rather than opening the lesson up to any type of influencer.

Short Lessons

The goal here was to cut the lesson time in half. We selected either the modeling or independent practice and condensed the hook and teaching parts of the lesson. This is a great option for when you need to blend the lesson into an existing unit or lesson in a specific subject. This version may also be a good place to start when first co-teaching.

Warm-up

This version of the lesson should last no more than five minutes and contain just the most essential concept or skill. Again, how you present the content is up to you, but we include a question or small activity.

Social Media/Announcement Posts

In this section, we provide suggestions for posts, videos, graphics, or series you can make with the digital citizenship content. If you are posting these to social media, this is a great time to switch the audience from students to adults and adjust the language to fit. For example, a post of screen time for students would sound different than a post on screen time for their guardians.

Asynchronous Suggestions

If the lesson content and design would work well taught asynchronously, we provided suggestions on how to present it. Often this is a playlist or choice board that can be turned in through a learning management system like Google Classroom or Canvas.

Resources

Not all the lessons have resources because links to these get outdated quickly. However, if a resource is integral to the lesson, we have included it here. For example, books for read-aloud or PDFs of official documents are cited here.

Lesson Title: One of These Things Is Not Like the Others: Internet Advertisements

Digital Citizenship Element: Digital Commerce (Ribble, 2015)

ISTE Standard: *2B—Students engage in positive, safe, legal, and ethical behavior when using technology, including social interactions online or when using networked devices.* (ISTE, 2021)

Level: Elementary

Full Lesson:

Section	Description
Hook or Anticipatory Set	• Find a clip of Toy Story 4: Woody meeting Duke Caboom for the first time. Duke Caboom tells the story of how his kid, Rejean, was disappointed that he as a toy could not perform the stunts the advertisement said he could. • Ask students if they remember a time where they wanted something based on an advertisement and when they got it, they were disappointed like Rejean was about Duke Caboom. (Discuss)
Objective/ Purpose	Students will learn what an online advertisement looks like and how marketing can use tricks or exaggeration to make goods/services seem appealing.
Teaching and Modeling/Guided Practice	Ask students: • Have you encountered advertisements online? • What is the purpose of an advertisement? • Where can you find advertisements on websites? (at the beginning of videos, in the middle of videos, on the sides of websites, in the middle of articles, etc.) Show students a few physical examples of products and the advertisements used to sell those products (example: board game commercials). Ask students: • Can you recognize that an ad is exaggerating? • What was different about the ad versus the actual product? • How might people who purchase this product be disappointed based on the advertisement? • Can you think of a time when an advertisement was accurate? • What made that advertisement different?

(Continued)

Section	Description
Independent Practice/ Check for Mastery	Practice analyzing advertisements for exaggeration and discuss with a partner what the reality of that product would be. Ask students to create an online ad that would accurately reflect the product being sold.
Materials Needed	A product that matches the advertisement
	A product that does not match the advertisement
	A few examples of toys/games and ads that sold them
	Example ads for students to analyze

Co-teach Lesson:

Co-teaching at the elementary level usually involves a full library lesson with support from the classroom teacher. In this lesson, I would utilize the teacher during independent practice, helping students analyze advertisements and making their advertisement that accurately reflects the product being sold.

Warm-up:

Display an Internet ad on a screen or in the students' Google Classroom/Canvas.

ASK:

- What is the ad selling?

- What does this ad promise?

- How might people who purchase this product be disappointed based on the advertisement?

Social Media/Announcement Posts:

Create a series of posts about online advertisements.

*What are they selling?

*Will the product reality match expectations?

*Will clicking the ad take you to a new website?

Lesson Title: You Don't Get Anything for Free

Digital Citizenship Element: Digital Commerce (Ribble, 2015)

ISTE Standard: *2D—Students manage their personal data to maintain digital privacy and security and are aware of data-collection technology used to track their navigation online.* (ISTE, 2021)

Level: Middle School

Full Lesson:

Section	Description
Hook or Anticipatory Set	• Display photos of the top 10 highest-paid YouTubers. • Ask if students are familiar with any of them. • Display how much revenue each of those YouTubers makes off of YouTube in a year. • Ask if they know how YouTubers make money.
Objective/ Purpose	Students will learn how their patronage of YouTubers' videos provides YouTubers with a paycheck, sponsors, and influence.
Teaching and Modeling/Guided Practice	Present information explaining how students' time, attention, interactions, and comments, provide YouTubers with money and fame. Think about the person you are spending time watching. They are earning money because you are watching. • Is this someone worthy of your time? • Do this person's values align with yours?
Independent Practice/ Check for Mastery	Give students a persuasive writing prompt: Persuade the teacher that a YouTuber of your choice is worth the teacher's time, attention, or interaction. Make sure you include the following in your persuasive writing: • YouTuber's name • Video content • Number of followers • Sponsors • Why should the teacher watch them? • Other important information that may persuade the teacher that the YouTuber is a good use of time and attention.
Materials Needed	Paper, writing material

Co-teach Suggestions:

This lesson connects well with English classes or as part of a debate prompt. This could also be used as a math lesson if you would like to have students calculate ad revenue.

Short Lesson:

Present information explaining how students' time, attention, interactions, and comments provide YouTubers with money and fame.

Think about the person you are spending time watching. They are earning money because you are watching.

- Is this someone worthy of your time?
- Do this person's values align with yours?

Warm-up:

Ask students to gather information about the top 10 highest-paid YouTubers.

- Find out how much revenue each of those YouTubers makes from YouTube in a year.
- Ask if they know how YouTubers make money.
- Have students decide if any of the YouTubers on their list is worth the student's time, attention, or interaction.

Social Media/Announcement Posts:

Who's making money because of you?

Create a series that sheds light on how Internet personalities make money from student use.

Lesson Title: More Stars Isn't Always Better

Digital Citizenship Element: Digital Commerce (Ribble, 2015)

ISTE Standard: *2D—Students manage their personal data to maintain digital privacy and security and are aware of data-collection technology used to track their navigation online.* (ISTE, 2021)

Level: High School

Full Lesson:

Section	Description
Hook or Anticipatory Set	Show students funny Amazon reviews and vote on the best ones. Ask students why they rated them high or low.
Objective/ Purpose	Students will analyze online reviews to better inform online purchases.

(Continued)

Section	Description
Teaching and Modeling/Guided Practice	Define and explain the following terms: • Verified purchase • Paid review
	Explain the pros and cons of different types of reviews and ratings such as: • Unboxing videos • Amazon review • Yelp ratings • Consumer Reports
Independent Practice/ Check for Mastery	Students research products or services to meet the needs of scenarios such as: • You got a new phone and need a new cover • Your cat broke their scratching post • You have a date and need to find a good restaurant Students must explain why they chose the product/service, including: • Sources they used to verify its quality • Short summaries of helpful reviews
Materials Needed	A device with Internet access

Co-teaching Suggestions:

This lesson would work well in an English class to practice analyzing for bias. It could also be adapted to teach in a math class by including price comparisons in the independent practice.

Short Lesson:

Explain the pros and cons of different types of reviews and ratings such as:

■ Unboxing videos

■ Amazon review

■ Yelp ratings

■ Consumer Reports

Students research a product or service of their choice and explain the following:

■ Sources they used to verify its quality

■ Short summaries of helpful reviews

Warm-up:

Show students a verified Amazon review and a bad review side by side. Have students write a response explaining the differences between the two reviews.

Social Media/Announcement Posts:

■ Share resources for quality product reviews

■ Share tips for spotting bad reviews

Lesson Title: Your Digital Identity

Digital Citizenship Element: Digital Communication (Ribble, 2015)

ISTE Standard: *2A—Students cultivate and manage their digital identity and reputation and are aware of the permanence of their actions in the digital world.* (ISTE, 2021)

Level: Elementary School

Full Lesson:

Section	Description
Hook or Anticipatory Set	Place footprints with different online company logos that your students enjoy visiting (YouTube, Nat Geo Kids, online gaming, etc.) throughout the library space. • Have students follow the trail of footprints, thinking about things they like from each platform. • Have students stop and pick up the nearest footprint and tell the class what they like to watch or do on that platform. • As a class, decide what you can infer about that student based on their favorite content. (They like animals, they like sports…)
Objective/ Purpose	Students will learn that everything they do or watch online is part of their digital footprint.
Teaching and Model- ing/Guided Practice	• Discuss the topic of digital footprint. • Discuss how each website they visit makes up their digital identity or adds to their digital footprint. • Discuss how subscribing to a channel on YouTube or another platform is part of your digital footprint.
Independent Practice/ Check for Mastery	• Give each child a footprint traced on paper. • Have them fill the footprint with words that make up a digital identity (who do they watch, what do they listen to, what type of videos attract them?) • When students are done, ask them to analyze the kind of person they are designing online.
Materials Needed	Paper, markers, crayons

Co-teach Lesson:

Co-teaching at the elementary level usually involves a full library lesson with support from the classroom teacher. In this case, I would utilize the teacher

during independent practice to help students figure out what kind of person ˌ
are designing online.

Warm-up:

Give each child a footprint traced on paper.

Have them fill it in with words that make up a digital identity (who do they watch, what do they listen to, what type of videos attract them?)

Social Media/Announcement Posts:

Digital footprint: The trail you leave behind online!

Create a series that helps students think about what kind of person they are designing online.

———————

Lesson Title: Defining Your Digital Self

Digital Citizenship Element: Digital Communication (Ribble, 2015)

ISTE Standard: *2A—Students cultivate and manage their digital identity and reputation and are aware of the permanence of their actions in the digital world.* (ISTE, 2021)

Level: Middle School

Full Lesson:

Section	Description
Hook or Anticipatory Set	Display these four words and have students write their definitions of each of them: • Positive • Permanence • Identity • Reputation Share the official definition of each of the words and have students react with how similar or different their definition is from the official definition. Ask students if these definitions change if we are using them in real life or as part of an online digital footprint.
Objective/ Purpose	Students cultivate and manage their digital identity and reputation and are aware of the permanence of their actions in the digital world.

(Continued)

Section	Description
Teaching and Modeling/Guided Practice	Your digital footprint is what represents you online. This could mean: • Photos you post/photos you like • Audio you post/audio you listen to • Videos you post/videos you listen to • Texts you send • "Likes" • Comments you post on friends' profiles Ask students to decide what they want their digital identity and reputation online to be and ask how they can start cultivating that digital footprint by things they post and share and by refraining from posting and sharing things that would put them in a bad light.
Independent Practice/ Check for Mastery	Choose a book character to make an online profile for. (This could also be adjusted to be a character from history, a type of biology term, weather pattern, etc.) Include: • Photos the character would post/photos the character would like • Audio the character would post/audio the character would listen to • Videos the character would post/videos the character would watch • Texts the character would send • "Likes" • Comments the character would post on friends' profiles.
Materials Needed	Computers, paper, writing material

Co-teach Lessons:

The possibilities for this co-teach lesson are endless. This could be used for an English class novel study, mythology studies, history/social studies classes for characters in history, or biology or other science classes as students make a profile for weather or types of bacteria/cells.

Warm-up:

Do an audit of your digital identity:

Your digital footprint is what represents you online. This could mean:

■ Photos you post/photos you like

■ Audio you post/audio you listen to

■ Videos you post/videos you listen to

- Texts you send
- "Likes"
- Comments you post on friends' profiles

Social Media/Announcement Posts:

Create a series of posts about digital footprint featuring the following words:

- Positive
- Permanence
- Identity
- Reputation

———————————

Lesson Title: Get LinkedIn to Your Digital Future

Digital Citizenship Element: Digital Communication (Ribble, 2015)

ISTE Standard: *2A—Students cultivate and manage their digital identity and reputation and are aware of the permanence of their actions in the digital world.* (ISTE, 2021)

Level: High School

Full Lesson:

Section	Description
Hook or Anticipatory Set	Have students Google themselves and answer the following questions: • What sites show up on the first-page search results? • What images are there of you? • What news stories are there of you? • Is there any personal information such as a phone number, address, etc.? • Is there anything an employer or college would find inappropriate?
Objective/ Purpose	Students will make a LinkedIn account to start curating their digital content and manage their digital reputation.
Teaching and Model-ing/Guided Practice	Discuss how high school students are creating LinkedIn profiles to get accepted to colleges and trade schools, as well as market themselves for jobs and internships.

(Continued)

Section	Description
	Discuss how to start adjusting your online image to be more professional: • Profile pictures • Email addresses • Audit of social media accounts
Independent Practice/ Check for Mastery	Students create a LinkedIn profile using content checklists from LinkedIn and other reputable sources. Some examples include: • Volunteering • Work experience • Honors and awards
Materials Needed	A device with Internet access

Co-teaching Suggestions:

This lesson works well in upper-level English, college prep, business, or marketing classes. Bringing in college counselors to help facilitate and provide feedback to students is also a great partnership for this lesson.

Short Lesson:

Students create a LinkedIn profile using content checklists from LinkedIn and other reputable sources. Some examples include:

■ Volunteering

■ Work experience

■ Honors and awards

Warm-up:

Have students Google themselves and answer the following questions:

■ What sites show up on the first-page search results?

■ What images are there of you?

■ What news stories are there of you?

■ Is there any personal information such as a phone number, address, etc.?

■ Is there anything an employer or college would find inappropriate?

Social Media/Announcement Posts:

■ Share posts about managing your online reputation

■ Share LinkedIn college checklist

Resources:

Michigan Technological University Career Services—LinkedIn—Networking And Interviews And Why It's Important: https://www.mtu.edu/career/students/networking/linkedin/.

Google—Manage your online reputation: https://support.google.com/accounts/answer/1228138?hl=en.

LinkedIn Profile Checklist—College Students: https://university.linkedin.com/content/dam/university/global/en_US/site/pdf /LinkedIn%20Profile%20Checklist%20-%20High%20School%20Students.pdf

Lesson Title: Building Good Screen Time Habits

Digital Citizenship Element: Digital Health and Wellness (Ribble, 2015)

ISTE Standard: *2B—Students engage in positive, safe, legal, and ethical behavior when using technology, including social interactions online or when using networked devices.* (ISTE, 2021)

Level: Elementary School

Full Lesson:

Section	Description
Hook or Anticipatory Set	Read *Unplugged* by Steve Antony or *When Charlie McButton Lost Power* by Suzanne Collins Discuss the story with students, asking what happened to the character when they were forced away from their screen.
Objective/ Purpose	Learning to limit screen time and build good screen time habits.
Teaching and Modeling/Guided Practice	Ask students: • What is screen time? • What do you like to do during screen time? • Is screen time good or bad? Make an anchor chart plan. How can you make sure you develop good screen time habits? • Ideas: Set a timer • Make meals screen-free • Put down your device when someone is talking to you—be present. • Plan other activities that make you happy so you don't fall into more screen time
Independent Practice/ Check for Mastery	What are good ways to spend screen time? • Fold a paper into three columns and have students label the columns where, when, and how • Have students illustrate (lower grade levels) or write (upper grade levels) their screen time plan: ○ Where will you use screens? ○ When can you use screens? ○ How can you use screens? Optional: On the back of the paper have students draw or write about their favorite nonscreen activity—share with the class.

(Continued)

Section	Description
Materials Needed	Paper, crayons, markers, chart paper, *Unplugged* by Steve Antony *When Charlie McButton Lost Power* by Suzanne Collins

Co-teach Suggestions:

Co-teaching at the elementary level usually involves a full library lesson with support from the classroom teacher. In this case, I would utilize a teacher to help with writing on the anchor chart and assisting students during independent practice.

Short Lesson:

Make an anchor chart plan:

How can you make sure you develop good screen time habits?

- Ideas: Set a timer.

- Make meals screen-free

- Put down your device when someone is talking to you—be present.

- Plan other activities that make you happy so you don't fall into more screen time.

Warm-up:

Make a plan to set healthy screen time limits:

Ask students to think about answers to the following questions and sketch their answers.

- Where can I use screens?

- When can I use screens?

- How can I use screens?

Social Media/Announcement Posts:

Create a series with ideas to build healthy screen time habits

Create a series of how students can make a plan to use screens

Examples:

- Where can I use screens (family room, car)?

- When can I use screens?

- How can I use screens?

Unplugged by Steve Antony

When Charlie McButton Lost Power by Suzanne Collins

Lesson Title: What Is the Science Behind the Screen?

Digital Citizenship Element: Digital Health and Wellness (Ribble, 2015)

ISTE Standard: *2B—Students engage in positive, safe, legal, and ethical behavior when using technology, including social interactions online or when using networked devices.* (ISTE, 2021)

Level: Middle School

Full Lesson:

Section	Description

Hook or Anticipatory Set	Have students estimate how long they spend online weekly.
	• If students have phones that show screen time usage, have them compare the time used to their estimate.
	• If students don't have phones, have them build a timeline of their online day. Have students estimate time spent online:
	  ○ Morning
	  ○ During the day
	  ○ Lunchtime
	  ○ After school
	  ○ In the evening
	  ○ Bedtime
	Have students come up with a weekly total based on their phone data or estimate.
	Ask: Are you surprised by your actual time spent online?

Objective/ Purpose	Students will learn why screens are attractive and how to develop good habits and boundaries around screen time that will help them step away from the screen.
Teaching and Modeling/Guided Practice	What is the science behind the screen? Present information on: • Dopamine • Blue light • Push notifications

(Continued)

Section	Description
Independent Practice/ Check for Mastery	Have students set goals to reduce screen time. • Reduce screen time by _____ minutes a day. • Reduce certain elements (social media, gaming) of screen time by _____ minutes a day. Screen time challenge: as a class set a goal to reduce screen time and have students log time or show screen time on phones. Challenge another class to lower their screen time too. Ask students to come up with a plan for what they are going to replace the screen time with. End of the week, students reflect: • What was hard about cutting down screen time? • What was easy about cutting down screen time? • What is something positive that came out of you cutting down screen time? • What advice do you have for peers about screen time now that you've limited yours?
Materials Needed	Paper, writing material, chart paper for goal setting, student devices (optional)

Co-teach Suggestions:

This lesson connects well with health classes or could be used as part of an English research paper. Work with the subject teacher to draw connections from mental health to the content currently being covered in class such as emotional health and development, psychological theories, or physical health.

Short Lesson:

What is the science behind the screen?

Present information on:

- Dopamine
- Blue light
- Push notifications

Warm-up:

Have students estimate how long they spend online weekly.

- If students have phones that show screen time usage, have them compare the time used to their estimate.

- If students don't have phones, have them build a timeline of their online day. Have students estimate time spent online:
  - Morning
  - During the day
  - Lunchtime
  - After school
  - In the evening
  - Bedtime

Have students come up with a weekly total based on their phone data or estimate.

Have students reflect on their reaction to the amount of screen time they spend.

Social Media/Announcement Posts:

Create a series of posts about the science of screen time. Explain the negative impact of too much screen time and give ideas to replace screen time habits.

Resources:

Savvy Cyber Kids—Why are screens so addictive?:
https://savvycyberkids.org/2021/01/13/why-are-screens-so-addictive/

Lesson Title: Leveling Up Mental Health

Digital Citizenship Element: Digital Health and Wellness (Ribble, 2015)

ISTE Standard: *2B—Students engage in positive, safe, legal, and ethical behavior when using technology, including social interactions online or when using networked devices.* (ISTE, 2021)

Level: High School

Full Lesson:

Section	Description
Hook or Anticipatory Set	Students rate how they are feeling using a mood meter. Then use a mindfulness app and have students complete a five-minute breathing exercise. After the exercise, have students rate their mood again and see if there was any change.

(Continued)

Section	Description
	The teacher then makes the connection that in our digital world there are many apps available to support people's health and wellness, including mental health, and users need to learn to choose them wisely.
Objective/ Purpose	Students will evaluate and choose credible mobile apps to support mental health and wellness.
Teaching and Modeling/Guided Practice	Teacher models using *One Mind PsyberGuide* to evaluate and select a mental health app. The following questions are answered by the teacher during modeling: *Why is this a credible website? Why is the disclaimer at the bottom of the website important? What area(s) of mental health am I exploring? What search limiters can I select to focus the search? What does each of the evaluation categories mean? What other resources are available to help learn about mental health?*
Independent Practice/ Check for Mastery	Students will choose a mental health topic and use the website *One Mind PsyberGuide* to choose three apps connected to that topic. The teacher will actively coach students through the practice by walking around the room and providing feedback. Once selected, students will submit their three choices and answer these questions about each one: *How does this app support mental health? Why do evaluators conclude that this is a good app? What is the scientific basis of this app?*
Materials Needed	• A device with access to the Internet • A mindfulness app • A journal or word processing program to record responses

Co-teaching Suggestions:

This lesson connects well with health, physical science, child development, or psychology classes. Work with the subject teacher to draw connections from mental health to the content currently being covered in class, such as emotional health and development, psychological theories, or physical health. Embedding this lesson in a larger research project on mental health or as a prompt for a design thinking project are other possibilities.

Short Lesson:

Students will choose a mental health topic and explore the website *One Mind PsyberGuide* to complete the following questions (this can be done digitally or on paper):

- Why is this a credible website for mental health apps?

- Why is the disclaimer at the bottom of the website important?

- What area(s) of mental health am I exploring?

- What search limiters can I select to focus the search on the topic?

- What does each of the evaluation categories mean?

- What is a highly rated app for this mental health topic?

Warm-up:

Students rate how they are feeling using a mood meter. Then have students complete a one-minute exercise on any mindfulness app. After the exercise, have students rate their mood again and see if there was any change. The teacher explains the value of mindfulness and how apps that use evidence-based practices can help support our health and wellness.

Social Media/Announcement Posts:

- Share specific apps for mental health and mindfulness

- Share resources from *One Mind Psyberguide*

- Share facts about mindfulness and mental health

Asynchronous Suggestion:

Create a video tutorial for navigating the *One Mind Psyberguide site*. Then embed formative assessment questions to check that students understand how to use the tool. This can be done with sites like Edpuzzle or using an online quiz maker like Google Forms. Then students will complete the independent practice and submit the answers digitally through a platform such as Google Classroom or Canvas.

Resources:

Edpuzzle:
https://edpuzzle.com/.

Speaking of Psychology: How To Choose Effective, Science-based Mental Health Apps With Stephen Schueller, Ph.D.: https://www.apa.org/research/action/speaking-of-psychology/science-based-mental-health-apps.

One Mind PsyberGuide:
https://onemindpsyberguide.org/.

Lesson Title: They're Copying Me!

Digital Citizenship Element: Digital Rights and Responsibilities (Ribble, 2015)

ISTE Standard: *2C Students demonstrate an understanding of and respect for the rights and obligations of using and sharing intellectual property.* (ISTE, 2021)

Level: Elementary School

Full Lesson:

Section	Description
Hook or Anticipatory Set	• Play a game of Simon Says. • Ask students to break down what Simon is asking them to do—copy him. • Discuss: Is copying someone a good thing or a bad thing? • Are there ways to copy someone and give them credit for their ideas?
Objective/ Purpose	Students will understand copyright and why citing sources is important.
Teaching and Modeling/Guided Practice	• Show students the copyright page in a book. • Explain that the copyright means that you cannot lawfully copy this person's work. • Explain the concept of intellectual property. Explain: • When you write or do a project, you can't copy someone's work without giving them credit for their ideas. All of the sources were created by someone and it is that person's intellectual property. • Not giving credit makes it seem like the ideas are your own. Stealing! • Using information from another person without giving them credit is called plagiarism. • Have students look at products, books, and websites for copyright symbols and information. Have them identify the copyright and explain what it means. Model how you cite a source. Note: For independent practice, students are going to do research and write four sentences about the topic they researched. One of the sentences is going to be directly from the source. Students are going to learn how to cite that source, so you may want to have your example be along the same lines as their research.

(Continued)

Section	Description
Independent Practice/ Check for Mastery	• Have students choose a topic to research. • Ask them to write four sentences about their research. • One of the sentences needs to come directly from the source to give their research authority. • Have students properly cite the source they used for their research.
Materials Needed	Books, computers, writing material, paper

Co-teach Lessons:

This lesson could be a full library lesson or could be used in connection with a classroom teacher's research unit. Plan with the classroom teacher to make sure the content of research aligns with what they are teaching in class.

Warm-up:

Have students look at products, books, and websites for copyright symbols and information. Have them identify the copyright and explain what it means.

Social Media/Announcement Posts:

Create a series of posts explaining how to cite sources and why it is important.

Lesson Title: Stitch This, Not That!

Digital Citizenship Element: Digital Rights and Responsibilities (Ribble, 2015)

ISTE Standard: *2C Students demonstrate an understanding of and respect for the rights and obligations of using and sharing intellectual property.* (ISTE, 2021)

Level: Middle School

Full Lesson:

Section	Description
Hook or Anticipatory Set	• Show example(s) of appropriate stitched videos on Tik Tok. • Have students explain what stitching is. • Is stitching copying someone? • Is stitching giving credit to the original poster?
Objective/ Purpose	Students will learn how to cite information and what options they have for copyright-free material on the Internet.

(Continued)

Section	Description
Teaching and Modeling/Guided Practice	Discuss the following: • Copyright • Creative Commons • Fair use • Citing • Imitation • Fanfiction Have students discuss what they can stitch and what they can't! Explain how to cite sources and how students can use citing websites to help them do it correctly.
Independent Practice/ Check for Mastery	Stitch This! Use Creative Commons to make a graphic or video about fair use.
Materials Needed	Computers

Co-teach Lessons:

This lesson can be embedded in any subject matter that is having students do research. Talk with the classroom teacher to align research topics with what they are teaching in class.

Warm-up:

Give students examples of properly cited and non-properly cited material. Have them decide if it is done correctly or not.

Social Media/Announcement Posts:

Create a series of posts about how to cite information.

Lesson Title: Everyone's an Influencer

Digital Citizenship Element: Digital Rights and Responsibilities (Ribble, 2015)

ISTE Standard: *2C Students demonstrate an understanding of and respect for the rights and obligations of using and sharing intellectual property.* (ISTE, 2021)

Level: High School

Section	Description
Hook or Anticipatory Set	Choose three students in your class and play the Two Truths and a Lie icebreaker game. Then show students a current event where social media influencers and companies were investigated for false advertising such as the Fyre Festival.
Objective/ Purpose	Students will understand and apply the FTC rules for social media influencers and sponsors.
Teaching and Model-ing/Guided Practice	• Explain why it is important that users know when they are being sold a product • Explain what the Federal Trade Commission is and why they exist • Share the FTCs Influencer Expectations
Independent Practice/ Check for Mastery	Students design a social media post or video for a product or service of their choice. The ad must follow all the FTC rules.
Materials Needed	• A device with Internet access • Camera • Green screen (optional) • Ring lights (optional)

Co-teaching Suggestions:

This lesson can be taught in any English class as part of a unit on persuasion. It also would work well as part of a debate or speech class by having students re-search and discuss the rights of influencers versus the rights of their followers.

Short Lesson:

Start by showing students a current event where social media influencers and companies were investigated for false advertising such as the Fyre Festival. Then explain why it is important that users know when they are being sold a product.

Students then design a social media post for a product or service of their choice. The ad must follow all the Federal Trade Commission (FTC) rules.

Warm-up:

Show students a current event where social media influencers and companies were investigated for false advertising such as the Fyre Festival. Then have students answer this question:

■ *Should influencers be required to tell their followers when a post is spon-sored or they are receiving compensation?*

Social Media/Announcement Posts:

- Share a graphic summarizing the FTC's influencer rules
- Share a list of expert influencers from different fields

Resources:

Federal Trade Commission—Disclosures 101 for Social Media Influencers: https://www.ftc.gov/tips-advice/business-center/guidance/disclosures-101-social -media-influencers.

Lesson Title: Is It Real or Fake?

Digital Citizenship Element: *Digital Literacy* (Ribble, 2015)

ISTE Standard: *2C Students demonstrate an understanding of and respect for the rights and obligations of using and sharing intellectual property.* (ISTE, 2021)

Level: Elementary School

Full Lesson:

Section	Description
Hook or Anticipatory Set	Read *The Donkey Egg* by Susan Stevens Crummel Was Fox a reliable source of information? What could Bear have done to verify information?
Objective/ Purpose	Students will learn how to use trustworthy sources to discern real information from fake information online.
Teaching and Model-ing/Guided Practice	Discuss the URL and what it can tell you. Use information from the resources provided or search for kid-friendly sites/graphics/videos that break down parts of a URL. Discuss the following six types of top-level domain suffixes and their meanings: .com .net .org .edu .gov .mil Discuss how to evaluate a website. Some examples to use (may differ by age group): 5 Ws of evaluating information RADAR framework CRAAP test Now that you've learned how to find trustworthy sources, use the "Did You Know" sections in *The Donkey Egg* to practice fact-checking using trustworthy sources.

(Continued)

Section	Description
Independent Practice/ Check for Mastery	What is the danger if we don't fact-check and verify information online? For lower grades: • Write a letter as a class to Bear telling him how he could avoid being fooled by Fox in the future and giving him good advice for online research. • Make a video for Bear with each student giving him good advice for online research. For upper grades: • Have students practice going to URLs .gov, .edu, and .org and reading the "about" sections. • Have students create a Venn diagram for things they see in common and differences they find among the different reliable websites.
Materials Needed	*The Donkey Egg* Susan Stevens Crummel Computers Paper, writing material

Co-teach Suggestions:

Co-teaching at the elementary level usually involves a full library lesson with support from the classroom teacher. In this case, I would utilize a teacher during independent practice to help with the class letter or video advice to Bear, or for upper grades, during students' investigation and comparison of uniform resource locators (URLs).

Short Lesson:

Discuss the URL and what it can tell you.

Use information from the resources provided or search for kid-friendly sites/graphics/videos that break down parts of a URL.

Discuss the following six types of top-level domain suffixes and their meanings:

.com

.net

.org

.edu

.gov

.mil

Discuss how to evaluate a website. Some examples to use (may differ by age group):

5 Ws of evaluating information

RADAR framework

CRAAP test

Warm-up:

- Create an "Is that a Fact?" series where you post strange facts and have students comment with a trustworthy source that proves or disproves that fact.
- Create an "Are you Trustworthy?" series where you post facts and have students choose who would be a trustworthy source to prove or disprove the fact.

Social Media/Announcement Posts:

- Create an "Is that a Fact?" series where you post strange facts and have users comment with a trustworthy source that proves or disproves that fact.
- Create an "Are you Trustworthy?" series where you post facts and have users choose who would be a trustworthy source to prove or disprove the fact.
- Create graphics that break down parts of a URL.
- Create graphics that explain the types of top-level domains

Asynchronous Lesson Ideas:

- Create an "Is that a Fact?" series where you post strange facts and have users comment with a trustworthy source that proves or disproves that fact.
- Create an "Are you Trustworthy?" series where you post facts and have students choose who would be a trustworthy source to prove or disprove the fact.

Resources:

Encyclopedia Britannica:
https://kids.britannica.com/students/article/domain-name/571189

Upstate University of South Carolina—Evaluating Information—STAAR Method: Website Evaluation:
https://uscupstate.libguides.com/c.php?g=257977&p=1721715

GCF Global: Understanding URLs
https://edu.gcfglobal.org/en/internetbasics/understanding-urls/1/

Indiana University Northwest—Library Skills Instruction: Website and Information Evaluation Criteria
https://libguides.iun.edu/libraryskillsinstruction/websiteevaluation

Loyola Marymount University: Evaluating Sources: Using the RADAR Framework
https://libguides.lmu.edu/aboutRADAR

The Donkey Egg by Susan Stevens Crummel and Janet Stevens

Lesson Title: Can You Spot a Fake?

Digital Citizenship Element: *Digital Literacy* (Ribble, 2015)

ISTE Standard: *2C Students demonstrate an understanding of and respect for the rights and obligations of using and sharing intellectual property.* (ISTE, 2021)

Level: Middle School

Full Lesson: Before you teach this lesson, you may want to review the *Washington Post*'s Fact Checker

Section	Description
Hook or Anticipatory Set	As technology advances, fake images and videos become harder to spot • Show students four or five photos that are obviously photoshopped—find silly pictures that couldn't happen without Photoshop (dogs flying planes). • Ask what clues help them know the photo is not real.
Objective/ Purpose	Students will learn how photos and videos can be altered/manipulated and how to use the information and online tools to discern authenticity.
Teaching and Modeling/Guided Practice	Ask students to think critically about photos and videos they see: • Where did this come from? • Do I know what the source is? • Does this make sense? Show some examples of doctored photos and manipulated videos. Introduce students to tools they can use online to help them verify the authenticity of photos/videos: • Google Reverse Image Search • InVID Verification • Check Light and Shadows – SunCalc • TinEye • YouTube DataViewer • Geolocation – Google Earth

(Continued)

Section	Description
	Older students:
	This video by the *Washington Post* Fact Checker explains how videos can be altered or manipulated and shows examples of videos that have been shared.
	https://www.youtube.com/watch?v=RVrANMAO7Sc
Independent Practice/ Check for Mastery	Give students videos and photos and have them analyze them for authenticity.
	Check mastery to see if they identified the bullet points:
	• Did this photo/video take place where it says it did? • What was the date this photo/video was created? • What is the source of this video? • How/why was this shared?
Materials Needed	Manipulated photos/videos, tabs open with different online tools discussed

Co-teach Lessons:

This lesson can be adapted to work with almost any subject because it can be narrowed down to fit the content—for example, social studies lessons on propaganda, politics, news stories, yearbook or newspaper classes about journalism, or English classes for media literacy content.

Warm-up:

Post a photo and have students evaluate.

Ask students to think critically about photos and videos they see.

■ Where did this come from?

■ Do I know what the source is?

■ Does this make sense?

Social Media/Announcement Posts:

Create a series in which you describe tools students can use online to help them verify the authenticity of photos/videos:

■ Google Reverse Image Search

■ InVID Verification

■ Check Light and Shadows – SunCalc

■ TinEye

- YouTube DataViewer
- Geolocation – Google Earth

Resources:

Common Sense Media—Reverse Google Image Search:
https://www.commonsense.org/education/videos/how-to-use-google-reverse
-image-search-to-fact-check-images

Poynter—10 Tips for Verifying Viral Social Media:
https://www.poynter.org/fact-checking/2018/10-tips-for-verifying-viral-social
-media-videos/

Washington Post—How to Spot a Fake Video:
https://www.washingtonpost.com/politics/2021/03/19/how-spot-fake-video/

Washington Post—Manipulated Video Guide:
https://www.washingtonpost.com/graphics/2019/politics/fact-checker
/manipulated-video-guide/h

Arizona State University—9 Tools to Identify Fake Images and Videos
https://newscollab.org/2019/02/04/9-tools-to-identify-fake-images-and
-videos/

Lesson Title: Are They an Influencer or Faker?

Digital Citizenship Element: *Digital Literacy* (Ribble, 2015)

ISTE Standard: *2C Students demonstrate an understanding of and respect for the rights and obligations of using and sharing intellectual property.* (ISTE, 2021)

Level: High School

Full Lesson:

Section	Description
Hook or Anticipatory Set	Read *The Donkey Egg* by Susan Stevens Crummel How is Fox like an Internet influencer? What tricks does Fox use against Bear? Why does Bear listen to Fox when he knows he is not reliable?
Objective/ Purpose	Students will evaluate social media influencers and rate them on their level of trustworthiness and validity.

(Continued)

Section	Description
Teaching and Modeling/Guided Practice	Students research an influencer of their choice and complete an influencer profile where they answer the following types of questions: • Name • Industry • Credentials • Social media platforms • Number of followers • Sponsors • Salary • What made them "influential" • How are they using their influence to affect the world? Students then post the finished profiles to a classroom discussion board or set them up as a gallery walk around the classroom.
Independent Practice/ Check for Mastery	Using the information from the profiles, students design their rating system for evaluating influencers. Then they design a product to share the rating system with others.
Materials Needed	A device with Internet access Slide deck program or graphic design program

Co-teaching Suggestions:

This lesson can be adapted to work with almost any subject because the influencer industries can be narrowed down to fit the content. For example, science classes could focus on fitness or medical influencers and history classes can focus on news influencers.

Short Lesson:

Students research an Influencer of their choice and complete an Influencer Profile where they answer the following types of questions:

- Name

- Industry

- Credentials

- Social Media Platforms

- Number of followers

- Sponsors

- Salary

- What made them "influential"
- How are they using their influence to affect the world?

Students then post the finished profiles to a classroom discussion board or set them up as a gallery walk around the classroom.

Warm-up:

Share a teacher made Influencer Profile and have students answer the following questions:

- Is this Influencer an expert in their industry? Why or why not?
- Does this Influencer positively or negatively affect culture? Why or why not?
- Are influencers an important part of our society? Why or why not?

Social Media/Announcement Posts:

- Share posts about credible influencers from different industries
- Share how to spot fake or bad influencers
- Share other places to fact check influencer content or recommendations

Resources:

Forbes' top influencers of 2017:
Forbes. https://www.forbes.com/top-influencers/#45fe269572dd.

USA Today *American Influencer Awards*:
https://www.aiaawards.com/.

The Donkey Egg by Susan Stevens Crummel and Janet Stevens

DIGITAL ETIQUETTE

Lesson Title: You Must Be Kind Online

Digital Citizenship Element: Digital Etiquette (Ribble, 2015)

ISTE Standard: *2B—Students engage in positive, safe, legal, and ethical behavior when using technology, including social interactions online or when using networked devices.* (ISTE, 2021)

Level: Elementary School

Full Lesson:

Section	Description
Hook or Anticipatory Set	Read *If You Plant a Seed* by Kadir Nelson Discuss the story: • What happened when the rabbit and mouse were unkind? • What happened when the rabbit and the mouse were kind?
Objective/ Purpose	Students will learn the importance of using kind and positive language online to interact with others.
Teaching and Modeling/Guided Practice	Discuss the word positive. How does it feel when people say positive things to you? Discuss the word negative. How does it feel when people say negative things to you? Play Thumbs Up/Thumbs Down: Show students positive and age-appropriate negative reviews of some of their favorite websites or shows. Ask students to compare positive and negative reviews. • Ask students how people who wrote negative reviews or posts could have responded differently or not at all. Give examples of things people post that students can practice commenting on; for lower grade levels the class as a whole could make a positive comment online: • A favorite YouTube artist • An Instagram post about your school • Nat Geo Kids article • The latest movie review they will relate to What are some examples of "seeds of kindness" that we can plant when we are online?

(Continued)

Section	Description
Independent Practice/ Check for Mastery	Have students (or the whole class) write a positive review of *If You Plant a Seed* to Kadir Nelson, the author. (Optional: Send it to him via Twitter.)
Materials Needed	*If You Plant a Seed* by Kadir Nelson Age-appropriate positive and negative posts of YouTube videos, websites students frequent, news stories, school reviews, etc. Paper, writing utensils Chart paper (younger grades)

Co-teach Lesson:

Co-teaching at the elementary level usually involves a full library lesson with support from the classroom teacher. In this case, I would utilize the teacher during Thumbs Up/Thumbs Down to help guide students to appropriate reactions and during independent practice having students write to Kadir Nelson individually for older grades and as a whole class for younger grades.

Warm-up:

Thumbs Up/Thumbs Down

Give students several examples of positive and negative posts/reviews.

Ask students:

- How do the following posts make you feel?

- Compare positive and negative reviews.

Social Media/Announcement Posts:

Plant seeds of kindness online and grow a garden!

Continue with the garden theme by having students weed negative words from positive ones or negative posts/reviews from positive posts/reviews.

Asynchronous Lesson:

Playlist:

Step 1: Read through the following positive reviews:

- YouTube videos

- Instagram posts

◻ Articles on Nat Geo Kids

◻ Articles on Nat Geo Kids

◻ Movie reviews

Step 2: What do you notice about all these posts?

Step 3: Why is it important to be kind?

Step 4: Practice writing a positive post to one of your favorite YouTubers here:

Lesson Title: You Make the Internet Safe

Digital Citizenship Element: Digital Etiquette (Ribble, 2015)

ISTE Standard: *2B—Students engage in positive, safe, legal, and ethical behavior when using technology, including social interactions online or when using networked devices.* (ISTE, 2021)

Level: Middle School

Full Lesson:

Section	Description
Hook or Anticipatory Set	Play a stop scrolling game. Prepare a mix of normal posts that students could read and scroll by and some troubling posts that may lead to someone being unsafe or a potentially dangerous situation. Have students respond to the post with either a hand signal for stop scrolling or a hand signal for keep scrolling.
	Ask students what made them choose to either stop or keep scrolling.
	Stop scrolling and say something: Explain to students that they need to tell a trusted adult if they come across anything online that:
	• Makes them feel uncomfortable
	• Makes them feel like they or another person is unsafe
	• Makes them feel a potential danger to themselves or others
Objective/ Purpose	Students will learn how to identify cyberbullying, suicide warning signs, and threats of violence online and what to do when they see it.
Teaching and Modeling/Guided Practice	Break students into groups and have them research how to identify and properly alert adults to cyberbullying, posts with suicidal thoughts, and threats of violence.

(Continued)

Section	Description
	This activity can either be done by having students jigsaw information and present it to the whole class or having students rotate through each station and choose which topic to present on.
	At each station supply QR codes that take students to age-appropriate websites about the following topics and/or books on the subject.
	Station 1: Cyberbullying
	Station 2: Suicide – the warning signs online
	Station 3: Threats of violence
	At each station ask students to research and answer the following questions:
	• Identify/define the topic.
	• Explain how the topics may look in the form of online posts.
	• Describe what a student who comes across information like this should do.
	• What are some likely outcomes of going to an adult with this information?
	• What are some consequences of not taking cyberbullying, suicidal thoughts, or threats of violence to an adult?
	• Make a plan: Who are trusted adults you could go to with this information:
	○ At school
	○ At home
	○ In the community
Independent Practice/ Check for Mastery	Have students make and present Stop Scrolling and Say Something! PSA videos or posters to the class and then display work around the school to spread awareness.
	Optional: Have students take a Stop Scrolling and Say Something! pledge to act when they see something online that concerns them. Have students sign the pledge and display it.
Materials Needed	Computers
	Books to use for research on the topics
	Paper, markers, pens
	Chart paper to make/sign the "Stop Scrolling and Say Something" pledge

Co-teach Lessons:

This lesson connects well with health or as part of research skills in English classes. Work with the subject teacher to draw connections from these topics to the content currently being covered in class such as emotional health and development or summarizing and paraphrasing information for research.

Embedding this lesson in a larger research project on mental health is another possibility.

Warm-up:

Display information that shows students that they need to tell a trusted adult if they come across anything online that:

- Makes them feel uncomfortable

- Makes them feel like they or another person is unsafe

- Makes them feel a potential danger to themselves or others

Make a plan: Who are trusted adults you could go to:

- At school

- At home

- In the community

Take a pledge: I pledge to Stop Scrolling and Say Something to make the Internet safe. I will report online posts to a trusted adult if the posts make me feel uncomfortable or unsafe, or if they have a threat of potential danger to others. I will make the Internet safe.

Social Media/Announcement Posts:

You make the Internet safe! Stop Scrolling and Say Something!

Create a series of posts that highlight what students can do if they come across information online that makes them feel uncomfortable or unsafe, or that have a threat of potential danger.

Asynchronous Lesson:

Make an online choice board where students can choose to become an expert on one of the following topics and make a slide deck of their research information to share with their teacher.

Topic 1: Cyberbullying

Topic 2: Suicide Prevention

Topic 3: Threats of Violence

You make the Internet safe! Learn how to respond when something makes you stop scrolling!

- Identify/define what each topic is.

- Explain how the topics may look in the form of online posts.

- Describe what a student who comes across information like this should do.

- What are some likely outcomes of going to an adult with this information?

- What are some consequences of not taking cyberbullying, suicidal thoughts, or threats of violence to an adult?

- Make a plan: Who are trusted adults you could go to with this information:

  □ At school

  □ At home

  □ In the community

Make a Plan:

Take a pledge: I pledge to Stop Scrolling and Say Something to make the Internet safe. I will report online posts to a trusted adult if the posts make me feel uncomfortable or unsafe, or if they have a threat of potential danger to others. I will make the Internet safe.

Resources:

Stopbullying.gov:
https://www.stopbullying.gov/resources/teens

Sandy Hook Promise:
https://www.sandyhookpromise.org/our-programs/say-something/

Lesson Title: When to Just Keep Scrolling

Digital Citizenship Element: Digital Etiquette (Ribble, 2015)

ISTE Standard: *2B—Students engage in positive, safe, legal, and ethical behavior when using technology, including social interactions online or when using networked devices.* (ISTE, 2021)

Level: High School

Full Lesson:

Section	Description
Hook or Anticipatory Set	Show students examples of mean posts about celebrities such as Jimmy Kimmel Live! Mean Tweets. Then explain how users could have reframed their tweet or kept scrolling and not engaged.
Objective/ Purpose	Students learn to protect their digital identity by not responding or creating content impulsively online.

(Continued)

Section	Description
Teaching and Modeling/Guided Practice	• Explain that even when comments or posts online are triggering, we do not have to respond. • Most of the time it is better to just keep on scrolling, but if you do feel you must respond, take a breath, walk away for an hour, and then type. • Never post while you are feeling a strong emotion, especially if you are upset. • The teacher then models how to edit a mean tweet with more appropriate language.
Independent Practice/ Check for Mastery	Students are given five mean tweets to rewrite with more appropriate language or content. Then have students post one of the tweets on a classroom discussion board and then respond to each other's tweets in an appropriate manner.
Materials Needed	A device with Internet access

Co-teaching Suggestions:

This lesson can be taught with any subject because learning to post and respond appropriately is an essential skill in any subject.

Short Lesson:

Students are shown an unedited mean tweet. Then the teacher models how to edit the tweet with more appropriate language.

Students are then given three mean tweets to rewrite with more appropriate language or content. Then have students post one of the tweets on a classroom discussion board and respond to each other's tweets in an appropriate manner.

Warm-up:

Show students examples of mean posts about celebrities such as Jimmy Kimmel Live! Mean Tweets. Then have students answer the question, "What should we do when we receive a mean tweet or comment from someone?"

Social Media/Announcement Posts:

■ Share posting alternatives like: "Keep scrolling!" or "Just delete!"

■ Share strategies for regulating emotions

■ Share an example of an original and an edited mean tweet

Conclusion

So often books on educational topics are heavy on theory and light on application, so we wrote these lesson plans to help provide ideas on *how* to implement digital citizenship in as many ways as possible. Whether your campus needs social media content, co-teach lessons, or read-aloud, we wanted to help inspire librarians to find a home for digital citizenship content in every aspect of our jobs. We also wanted to show how to vertically align digital citizenship concepts across grade levels, so that the content complexity grows with students. Our digital world is complex, and we have to dig into content that is appropriate for our students both emotionally and intellectually. It can also be frustrating because creating digital citizenship lessons is like buying a new car; they depreciate the moment you drive off the lot. However, we hope that these lessons, and ultimately this book, equip librarians with the tools and planning processes necessary to create new lessons that reflect our constantly changing digital world.

Appendix A: Sample Lateral Reading Program

Description: *What is a lateral reader and how do you become one? Why should you be?*

In order to confirm the validity of a source—website, news source, etc.—instead of just analyzing the site itself, you need to take a look at what others say about that source. You can look at a source and think it is valid, trustworthy, or legitimate based on appearance alone, but until you have vetted that source by seeing how others regard it, you can't know how trustworthy it really is.

Digital Citizenship Element: Digital communication/media literacy

ISTE Standards: *3a: Students plan and employ effective research strategies to locate information and other resources for their intellectual or creative pursuits. 3b: Students evaluate the accuracy, perspective, credibility and relevance of information, media, data or other resources.*

Example: You follow your city's local news on Twitter, so you already feel that they are a trusted source. When reading or searching about a particular subject, you will go to your local news because in your mind, you have already confirmed it is a reliable and trusted source. However, if you haven't actually confirmed the local news is reliable, well-respected, and contains facts without bias, then you are getting all of your information from an unreliable source.

Materials:

- Paper and pencils
- Printed copies of example news articles
- Worksheet

Instruction:

1. Talk about bias and how our backgrounds, past experiences, culture, family, where we get our information, and much more all inform our biases.

2. Discuss what our own biases are. Think about where you get your information.

3. Describe the concept of lateral reading.

4. Conduct the Google Activity that follows.

Discussion:

1. What are your biases?

2. Where do you get your information from?

3. What are some new places you can get your information?

4. Why is it important to know the reliability of a source instead of searching something online?

5. Did you get different answers than other people?

6. Was there something new you learned from looking at a different response to the same keyword?

Search for a subject or keyword and write the top five search results, as well as the first snippet that shows up:

Keyword: _____

1.

2.

3.

4.

5.

Keyword: _____

1.

2.

3.

4.

5.

Appendix B: Sample Program for Teaching Copyright Law to Elementary-Aged Students

Description: This activity teaches younger children the basics of copyright and the concept of digital ethics. Digital ethics means treating people respectfully and kindly online. A copyright is the legal protection given to the creator of a work. This can include things like books, art, music, movies, and more.

Digital Citizenship Element: Digital law, digital rights and responsibilities

ISTE Standard: *2c: Students demonstrate an understanding of and respect for the rights and obligations of using and sharing intellectual property.*

Instructions:

1. Describe to the children what copyright means.

2. Describe to the children what digital ethics means.

3. Pass out paper and writing utensils to the class.

4. Encourage your students to draw a picture of something they care about.

5. Lead the students in a discussion around ethics and copyright.

Discussion:

- The art you drew belongs to you, not anyone else. This is like copyright. How would you feel if someone else tried to take your art?

- How would you feel if someone took your art and scribbled on it? Can it be repaired?

- How can we respect other people's creations online?

Appendix C: Sample Social Media Policy

Introduction/Purpose: Libraries should write here how they define social media and give examples. Reference the mission of the library and how it relates to the social media guideline. For example, if the library mission includes something like, "We aspire to spark curiosity in our patrons," use the word "curiosity" in defining the goals of the social media policy.

Rules: Reference any HR rules that pertain to the library. This can include links to privacy policies, employee conduct, and more. Rules of how often to communicate should be entered here, as well as speech that is not allowed per HR policy. Moderating policies can also be incorporated here.

Guides/Best Practices: This can include a digital etiquette guideline. It also should reference the goals of the policy. In this section write what the library wants to see. This is a space where recommended practices such as courtesy, respect, and transparency can be further defined and elaborated upon.

Other: Consider linking to references at the end of the policy that informed the rules and goals. These can be links to other social media policies the library pulled ideas from. Also, include a list of other policies in the school district, county, city, or other organizations such as the American Library Association that guide the library. Make sure to write when the policy was created and when it was last updated.

Appendix D: Sample Minecraft Mentor Program for Teens

Description: Minecraft is a popular program from young children to adults. As young children start playing on their own, the guidance and mentorship of teens can help teach them how to play and help them play safely. Peer mentors can help set up accounts, manage mods, introduce the younger person to crafting and the various rules, and be someone they can ask questions of and befriend. These Minecraft mentors can also guide and support younger students if they are dealing with any cyberbullying or other online harassment.

Digital Citizenship Elements: Digital security/online safety, digital etiquette and digital literacy

ISTE Standard: *1d: Students understand the fundamental concepts of technology operations, demonstrate the ability to choose, use and troubleshoot current technologies and are able to transfer their knowledge to explore emerging technologies.*

Note: Minecraft Education offers a mentor program certified badge and courses such as a Teacher Academy to assist in mentorship. For libraries that have active Minecraft programs, this may be a way for librarians to be better trained on delivering the programs and training peer mentors.

How To:

1. Get buy-in from administration to start a new mentorship program. If an existing Minecraft club or regular library program already exists, mentorship programs can be added.

2. Recruit and market to teens to be Minecraft mentors. After teens are recruited, have them agree to guidelines around what mentors do and don't do.

3. Offer the Minecraft teen mentors at specific and regular times at the library. Target upper elementary students as the ones to be mentored. Since this program may be noisier with more conversation back and forth, consider setting up separate computers or space for it.

4. Regularly check in with the mentors and the mentees. Find ways to encourage, motivate, and even reward consistent mentors.

Appendix E: Sample Digital Parenting Event

Description: Parents and caregivers are essential partners to building digital citizens. They can reinforce the learning at the school and the library at home. Parents also are students of digital citizenship and can be taught these concepts through the library.

Digital parenting events can be virtual, in person, and at varying times depending on the schedule of the audience. Consider having a digital parenting event at the same time other parenting events may be happening at your organization. Try to keep the event at 90 minutes or less.

Digital Citizenship Elements: Varies, but many digital parent events include the elements of digital literacy (i.e., how to use devices, change settings) and digital security/online safety.

Set-up:

- Computer/projector
- Tables and chairs
- Resources/book display on digital citizenship topics
- Devices (optional if you are teaching how to use a device)
- Food (optional)
- Prizes/incentives (optional)

How To:

1. Advertise with existing partners and give enough notice. Consider providing food/snacks at the event. Mention the event in newsletters, displays, social media, and more.

2. Start off by having a discussion with the parents about their thoughts and concerns around technology in the home. You can also split up parents into small groups to discuss the topic.

3. Define digital citizenship and all the parts to keeping children safe and responsible online. Have them examine ways they can be an active participant with technology and their children.

4. When presenting, be more of a guide and moderator to the parents than a lecturer. Ask the parents their suggestions and thoughts and give them time to respond and share any concerns they have. Build in additional time for questions and discussions.

5. If the library is hosting someone else to come in, help provide support for the event and advertise.

References

American Academy of Pediatrics (AAP). (2019, November 12). *Healthy digital media use habits for babies, toddlers & preschoolers.* HealthyChildren .org https://www.healthychildren.org/English/family-life/Media/Pages /Healthy-Digital-Media-Use-Habits-for-Babies-Toddlers-Preschoolers .aspx

American Association of School Librarians (AASL). (2021, January 11). *Home.* National School Library Standards. https://standards.aasl.org/

American Library Association (ALA). (1996, January 23). *Library bill of rights.* Advocacy, Legislation & Issues. https://www.ala.org/advocacy /intfreedom/librarybill

American Library Association (ALA). (2018, May 23). *Privacy policy.* Home. https://www.ala.org/privacypolicy

American Library Association (ALA). (2019, June 24). *Privacy: An interpretation of the library bill of rights.* Advocacy, Legislation & Issues. https://www .ala.org/advocacy/intfreedom/librarybill/interpretations/privacy

American Library Association (ALA). (2019, July 13). *First amendment and censorship.* Advocacy, Legislation & Issues. http://www.ala.org/advocacy /intfreedom/censorship

American Library Association (ALA). (2020, June 1). *The freedom to read statement.* Advocacy, Legislation & Issues. http://www.ala.org/advocacy /intfreedom/freedomreadstatement

American Library Association (ALA). (2021, February 25). *Resolution in opposition to facial recognition software in librarie*s. Advocacy, Legislation & Issues. http://www.ala.org/advocacy/intfreedom /facialrecognitionresolution

Anderson, M., & Horrigan, J. B. (2016). *Smartphones may not bridge digital divide for all.* Pew Research Center. http://www.pewresearch.org/fact -tank/2016/10/03/smartphones-help-those-without-broadband-get -online-but-dont-necessarily-bridge-the-digital-divide/

Anythink Libraries. (2014, August 5). *Discussion guidelines.* https://www .anythinklibraries.org/about/policies/discussions

Association for Library Services for Children. (n.d.). *Home page.* Every child ready to read. Read. Learn. Grow. http://everychildreadytoread.org/

Better Business Bureau. (2020, January 28). BBB tip: Writing an effective privacy policy for your business' website. *BBB.* https://www.bbb.org/article/news -releases/21390-bbb-tip-writing-an-effective-privacy-policy-for-your -small-business-website

Bloom, B. S. (1970). *Taxonomy of educational objectives. The classification of educational goals.* Longman.

Bond, S. (2021, April 26). *Parler's new iPhone app will block posts that Apple prohibits.* NPR. https://www.npr.org/2021/04/26/990792665 /parlers-new-iphone-app-will-block-posts-that-apple-prohibits

Boston Public Library. (n.d.). *Homework assistance program.* Boston Public Library. https://www.bpl.org/homework-help-for-grades-k-8/

Breeding, M. (2019, October 25). *Personalization vs. privacy.* American Libraries Magazine. https://americanlibrariesmagazine.org/2019/11/01/personalization-vs-privacy/

Bulao, J. (2021, May 18). *How much data is created every day in 2021? [You'll be shocked!].* TechJury. https://techjury.net/blog/how-much-data-is-created-every-day/

Busby, J., Tanberk, J., & Cooper, T. (2021, May 27). *BroadbandNow estimates availability for all 50 states; confirms that more than 42 million Americans do not have access to broadband.* BroadbandNow. https://broadbandnow.com/research/fcc-broadband-overreporting-by-state

Chicago Public Library (CPL). (2018, April 27). *On the table: Meet. Share. Do.* CPL. https://www.chipublib.org/news/on-the-table-meet-share-do/.

Choose Privacy Every Day. (2021, June 11). *Voices for privacy blog.* American Library Association. https://chooseprivacyeveryday.org/

Common Sense Media. (2019). Media use by tweens and teens 2019: Infographic. *Common sense media.* Common Sense Media: Ratings, reviews, and advice. https://www.commonsensemedia.org/Media-use-by-tweens-and-teens-2019-infographic. Accessed February 21, 2021.

Cornell University Library. (n.d.). *Copyright term and the public domain in the United States.* Copyright Information Center. https://guides.library.cornell.edu/copyright/publicdomain

Cortesi, S., Hasse, A., Lombana-Bermudez, A., Kim, S., & Gasser, U. (2020). *Youth and digital citizenship+ (plus): Understanding skills for a digital world.* Berkman Klein Center for Internet & Society.

Coward, C., McClay, C., & Garrido, M. (2018). Public libraries as platforms for civic engagement. In *Seattle: Technology & social change group* (pp. 11, 14–16). University of Washington Information School.

Daws, R. (2020, May 28). Smart speaker usage increases substantially due to COVID-19 quarantines. *Internet of Things News.* https://iottechnews.com/news/2020/may/01/smart-speaker-usage-increases-covid-19-quarantines/

Delgado, E. (2020). Libraries as third spaces for children. *Public Libraries, 59*(5), 44–49.

District of Columbia Public Library (DCPL). (2021, May 19). *Civic engagement 101 summer session: Let's talk about race.* DCPL. https://www.dclibrary.org/node/68124

Electronic Frontier Foundation. (2021, April 27). *HTTPS everywhere.* EFF. https://www.eff.org/https-everywhere

Electronic Frontier Foundation. (n.d.). *Surveillance self-defense.* https://ssd.eff.org/

Federal Communications Commission (FCC). (2020, September 16). *E-rate: Universal service program for schools and libraries.* https://www.fcc.gov/consumers/guides/universal-service-program-schools-and-libraries-e-rate

Federal Trade Commission (FTC). (2019, November 20). *Google and YouTube will pay record $170 million for alleged violations of children's privacy law.* https://www.ftc.gov/news-events/press-releases/2019/09/google-youtube-will-pay-record-170-million-alleged-violations

Free Privacy Policy. (2020, December 28). *Where to place your privacy policy on your website and app.* https://www.freeprivacypolicy.com/blog/privacy-policy-placement/

Fung, B. (2021, January 9). Twitter bans President Trump permanently. *CNN.* https://www.cnn.com/2021/01/08/tech/trump-twitter-ban/index.html

Gaines, L. V. (2019, May 14). *Local libraries look to combat 'fake news' with media literacy programs.* chicagotribune.com. https://www.chicagotribune.com/suburbs/highland-park/ct-hpn-librarians-fake-news-education-tl-0309-20170306-story.html

Gholipour, B. (2018, January 18). *We need to open the AI black box before it's too late.* Futurism. https://futurism.com/ai-bias-black-box

Gray, A. (2016, November 8). *Freedom of speech: Which country has the most?* World Economic Forum. https://www.weforum.org/agenda/2016/11/freedom-of-speech-country-comparison/

Hathaway, B. (2021). Domo releases eighth annual "Data Never Sleeps" infographic. *Business Wire.* https://www.businesswire.com/news/home/20200811005135/en/

Harvard University. (2020, January 27). *Serve and return.* Center on the Developing Child at Harvard University. https://developingchild.harvard.edu/science/key-concepts/serve-and-return/

Hunter, R., & Hunter, M. C. (2004). *Madeline Hunter's mastery teaching: Increasing instructional effectiveness in elementary and secondary schools.* Corwin Press.

International Society for Technology in Education (ISTE). (2021). *ISTE standards for students.* ISTE. https://www.iste.org/standards/for-students

International Society for Technology in Education (ISTE). (n.d.). *DigCit commit.* DigCitCommit. https://digcitcommit.org/

Jacobson, L. (2019, November 5). *US students show low-to-medium tech skills.* K-12 Dive. https://www.k12dive.com/news/students-show-low-to-medium-tech-skills/566498/

Kalia, A., & McSherry, C. (2015, November 22). *Viacom v. YouTube.* Electronic Frontier Foundation. https://www.eff.org/cases/viacom-v-youtube

Kennedy, B., Fry, R., & Funk, C. (2021, April 14). *6 facts about America's STEM workforce and those training for it.* Pew Research Center. https://www.pewresearch.org/fact-tank/2021/04/14/6-facts-about-americas-stem-workforce-and-those-training-for-it/

Knight Foundation. (2020, August 4). *American views 2020: Trust, media and democracy.* https://knightfoundation.org/reports/american-views-2020-trust-media-and-democracy/

Knight Foundation. (2022, March 9). *Media and democracy: Unpacking America's complex views on the Digital Public Square.* https://knightfoundation.org/reports/media-and-democracy/

Kranich, N. (2012). *Library and book trade almanac* (essay; pp. 79, 88–89). Information Today, Inc.

Lebow, S. (2022, April 7). *A not-so-smart rise for smart speaker ownership.* Insider Intelligence. https://www.emarketer.com/content/smart-speaker-ownership

Lemon, J. (2021, January 11). Angela merkel calls Trump Twitter ban problematic as freedom of opinion is fundamental right. *Newsweek*. https://www.newsweek.com/angela-merkel-calls-trump-twitter-ban-problematic-freedom-opinion-fundamental-right-1560562

Library Freedom Project. (n.d.). *We fight surveillance*. Library Freedom. https://libraryfreedom.org/

Library of Congress. (n.d.). Constitution day teacher resources. https://www.loc.gov/classroom-materials/constitution-day-resources/

Lombana, A., Cortesi, S., Fieseler, C., Gasser, U., Hasse, A., Newlands, G., & Wu, S. (2020, June 25). *Youth and the digital economy: Exploring youth practices, motivations, skills, pathways, and value creation*. Berkman KleinCenter. https://cyber.harvard.edu/publication/2020/youth-and-digital-economy

Madigan, S., Browne, D., Racine, N., Mori, C., & Tough, S. (2019). Association between screen time and children's performance on a developmental screening test. *JAMA Pediatrics*, *173*(3), 244–250. doi:10.1001/jamapediatrics.2018.5056

McCulloch, G. (2020). *Because internet: Understanding the new rules of language*. Thorndike Press, a part of Gale, a Cengage Company.

McElrath, K. (2020, August 26). *Schooling during the Covid-19 pandemic*. The United States Census Bureau. https://www.census.gov/library/stories/2020/08/schooling-during-the-covid-19-pandemic.html

Mehrabian, A., & Weiner, M. (1967). Decoding of inconsistent communications. *Journal of Personality and Social Psychology*, *6*(1), 109–114.

MENTOR. (n.d.). *Peer mentoring supplement*. Peer Mentoring. https://www.mentoring.org/wp-content/uploads/2020/08/Peer-Mentoring-Supplement-to-the-EEP_Summary.pdf

Merriam-Webster. (n.d.). *'Getting Canceled' and 'Cancel Culture': What it means*. Merriam-Webster. https://www.merriam-webster.com/words-at-play/cancel-culture-words-were-watching

Metz, C. (2020, October 29). Twitter bots poised to spread disinformation before election. *The New York Times*. https://www.nytimes.com/interactive/2020/10/29/technology/election-twitter-trump-biden.html

Monterosa, V. (2021). Digital citizenship for education leaders. *Leadership Magazine*. https://leadership.acsa.org/digital-citizenship-for-education-leaders

Mossberger, K., Tolbert, C. J., & McNeal, R. S. (2008). *Digital citizenship: The internet, society, and participation*. Cambridge, MA: The MIT Press.

NAMLE. (2020). *Snapshot 2019: The state of media literacy education in the U.S.* National Association for Media Literacy Education. https://namle.net/wp-content/uploads/2020/10/SOML_FINAL.pdf

National Digital Inclusion Alliance (NDIA). (2020, September 24). *Definitions*. NDIA. https://www.digitalinclusion.org/definitions/

National Governors Association Center for Best Practices and Council of Chief State School Officers. (n.d.). *English language arts standards*. English Language Arts Standards | Common Core State Standards Initiative. http://www.corestandards.org/ELA-Literacy/

Nead, N. (2020, October 5). *The problem with defining bad algorithms in software development*. ReadWrite. https://readwrite.com/2020/10/05/the-problem -with-defining-bad-algorithms-in-software-development/

Nguyen, Kevin A., Borrego, Maura, Finelli, Cynthia J., DeMonbrun, Matt, Crockett, Caroline, Tharayil, Sneha, Shekhar, Prateek, Waters, Cynthia, & Rosenberg, Robyn. (2021). Instructor strategies to aid implementation of active learning: A systematic literature review. *International Journal of STEM Education, 8*, 9. https://doi.org/10.1186/s40594-021 -00270-7

Nonprofit Technology Network (NTEN). (2021, May 20). *Digital inclusion fellowship*. NTEN. https://www.nten.org/major-initiatives/dif/

Pahwa, N. (2020, August 7). What Indians lost when their government banned TikTok. *Slate Magazine*. https://slate.com/technology/2020/08/tiktok -india-ban-china.html.

Pappas, S. (2020, April 1). *What do we really know about kids and screens?* Monitor on Psychology. https://www.apa.org/monitor/2020/04/cover -kids-screens

Petska, A. (2018, August 31). Roanoke County library adds Pepper, a 'community robot'. *Roanoke Times*. https://roanoke.com/news/local/roanoke-county -library-adds-pepper-a-community-robot/article_198827e4-e357-545a -9f14-2e8137f83208.html

Pew Research Center. (2020, November 30). *How much broadband speed do Americans need?* How Much Broadband Speed Do Americans Need | The Pew Charitable Trusts. https://www.pewtrusts.org/en/research-and-analysis /articles/2020/11/30/how-much-broadband-speed-do-americans-need

Pugmire, G. (2020, September 23). Digital inequity in Utah County, united way helping. *Daily Herald*. https://www.heraldextra.com/news/local/central /provo/digital-inequity-in-utah-county-united-way-helping/article _3299ebaf-7ba8-525f-88a6-8a49b69de661.html

Rainie, L. (2017, April 3). *The secret mission that people yearn to have libraries address*. Pew Research Center: Internet, Science & Tech. https://www.pewresearch.org/internet/2017/04/03/the-secret-mission -that-people-yearn-to-have-libraries-address/

Ribble, M. (2015). *Digital citizenship in schools* (3rd ed.). Eugene, OR: International Society for Technology in Education.

Richter, F. (2020, January 9). *Infographic: Smart speaker adoption continues to rise*. Statista Infographics. https://www.statista.com/chart/16597/smart -speaker-ownership-in-the-united-states/

Rideout, V., & Robb, M. B. (2020). *The common sense census: Media use by kids age zero to eight*. San Francisco, CA: Common Sense Media.

Roanoke County VA Government Website. (n.d.). *Pepper, the humanoid robot*. Roanoke County VA Library. https://www.roanokecountyva.gov/2046/Pepper

Rogers-Whitehead, C. (2016, August 24). *Seniors get tutored in technology by teens*. KSL.com. https://www.ksl.com/article/41183763

Rogers-Whitehead, C. (2019). *Digital citizenship: Teaching strategies and practice from the field*. Rowman & Littlefield.

Rogers-Whitehead, C. (2019, December 17). *Is your workplace spying on you?* Utah Business. https://www.utahbusiness.com/workplace-spying/

Rogers-Whitehead, C. (2020, February 3). *Updating the 5Ws for a new media literacy.* Connected Learning Alliance. https://clalliance.org/blog/updating-the-5ws-for-a-new-media-literacy/

Rogers-Whitehead, C. (2021, February 26). *How educators can use discord to connect with students.* ISTE. https://www.iste.org/explore/tools-devices-and-apps/how-educators-can-use-discord-connect-students

Schulte, L. (2014, July 15). *Common core state standards—Resources.* Association for Library Service to Children (ALSC). https://www.ala.org/alsc/ccss-resources

Simon, H. A. (1971). *Designing organizations for an information-rich world* (pp. 37–52). Johns Hopkins University Press. Retrieved 28 October 2020. Accessed May 17, 2021. https://www.scribd.com/document/490917904/Designing-Organizations-for-an-Information-Rich-World

Solomon, M. R., Poatsy, M. A., & Martin, K. (2016). *Better business* (Vol. 4). Pearson.

Tomlinson, C. A. (2014). *The differentiated classroom: Responding to the needs of all learners* (2nd ed.). Pearson Education, Inc., by special arrangement with the Association for Supervision and Curriculum Development (ASCD).

Udell, E. (2020, November 2). *Let them lead.* American Libraries Magazine. https://americanlibrariesmagazine.org/2020/11/02/let-them-lead-teen-activism/

Urban Libraries Council. (n.d.). *Leadership brief: Libraries leading AI and digital citizenship.* Urban Libraries Council. https://www.urbanlibraries.org/files/AI_Leadership-Brief.pdf

UserWay. Inc., U. W. (n.d.). *WCAG 2.1 & ADA compliance.* WCAG 2.1 & ADA Compliance | Web Accessibility is UserWay. https://userway.org/

Waltham Public Library. (n.d.). *Real talk.* https://sites.google.com/minlib.net/real-talk-teens/home

Wojcicki, S. (2019, September 4). *An update on kids and data protection on YouTube.* blog.youtube. https://blog.youtube/news-and-events/an-update-on-kids

Index

About the Authors

Carrie Rogers-Whitehead worked for public libraries for a decade before founding Digital Respons-Ability, a mission-based company that works with educators, parents, and students to teach digital citizenship. Her company provides training to tens of thousands of students, parents, and educators across her state of Utah and beyond. Carrie is also the author of *Digital Citizenship: Teaching Strategies and Practice from the Field* and several academic titles, including the ABC-CLIO publication *Serving Teens and Adults on the Autism Spectrum: A Guide for Libraries*, which was a recipient of the 2021 Outstanding Reference Source List from the American Library Association.

Amy O. Milstead is a library media specialist at Vanguard High School in Mesquite, Texas. This is her seventeenth year in public education, where she has taught fourth grade, sixth grade, and special education and has been an elementary, middle, and high school librarian/media specialist. She has served on committees and presented at the Texas Librarian Association conference. Milstead played a role in Mesquite Independent School District's winning of the American Association of School Libraries Library Program of the Year Award. This is her first professional book publication.

Lindi Farris-Hill is a library media specialist at Mesquite High School in Mesquite, Texas. With more than a decade of experience in public education, Farris-Hill has also worked as a district instructional technology coach and a high school English teacher. She is an active member and presenter at both the Texas Library Association and the Texas Computer Educators Association annual conferences. In 2020, Farris-Hill played a role in Mesquite Independent School District's winning of the American Association of School Librarians' Library Program of the Year Award. This is her first professional book publication.